Discov

BRIAN ABBS · INGRID FREEBAIRN

STUDENTS' BOOK 1

Longman

Contents

LANGUAGE USE	LANGUAGE

LESSON 1 Hello.

Say hello	Hello.
Ask and say your name	What's your name?
	My name's....
Count to ten	1, 2, 3 etc.

LESSON 2 Good morning.

Greet people formally	Good morning/afternoon/evening.
Introduce yourself	I'm Mr Green.
	I'm Andy's teacher.
Say goodbye	Goodbye.

LESSON 3 This is my family.

Greet people you know	Hello. How are you?
	I'm OK, thanks.
Say hello informally	Hi!
Introduce people	This is Sue.
Identify people	She's a friend from school.
Say yes and no	Yes! No!
Give orders	Go away, Lucy.

LESSON 4 He's called Big Ben.

Ask and talk about names	What's her name?
	Her name's Cleopatra.
	She's called Cleo.
Ask and identify people by name	Who's that?
	That's Prince Charles.
Say goodbye informally	I must go. Bye.

LESSON 5 Roundup

LESSON 6 How old are you?

Ask and say your age	How old are you?
	I'm eleven (years old).
	Are you eleven?
	Yes I am./No, I'm not.
	I'm twelve.
	I'm nearly six.
Count to twenty	11, 12, 13 etc.

LESSON 7 What's your address?

Ask and give addresses and telephone numbers	What's your address?
	It's 65, Cliff Road.
	What's your telephone number?
Count to 100	20, 30, 40 etc.

LANGUAGE USE	LANGUAGE

LESSON 8 What's this?

Ask about and identify objects	What's this/that?
	Is it a ruler?
	Yes, it is./No, it isn't.
	It's a calculator.

LESSON 9 It's an African elephant.

Identify animals	It's an African elephant.
Ask and say where animals are from	Where is it from?
	It's from Africa.
	This eagle is from North America.

LESSON 10 Roundup

LESSON 11 He's American.

Ask about and identify people	Who's that man?
	That's Harrison Ford.
Ask and say where people are from	Where's he from?
	He's from the USA.
Ask and talk about nationality	Is he British?
	Yes, he is./No, he isn't.
	He's American.
	What nationality are you?
	I'm Spanish.

LESSON 12 We're from Penzance.

Ask and talk about nationality	Are you/they Japanese?
	Yes, we/they are.
	No, we/they aren't.
	We're German.
	We're from Germany.
Warn people	Look out!
Apologise	Sorry!
Accept apologies	That's OK.
	It doesn't matter.

LESSON 13 Do you want a sweet?

Offer things	Do you want a sweet?
Accept and refuse	Yes, please./No, thank you.
Give things	Here you are.
Say what you like and don't like	I love crisps.
	I hate liquorice.
Thank people for things formally and informally	Thank you very much.
	Thanks for the sweet.
Accept thanks	That's OK.

LANGUAGE USE	LANGUAGE
LESSON 14 What colour are your eyes?	
Ask and talk about hair and eye colour	What colour is his hair/are your eyes? It's brown./They're blue.
Ask and talk about favourite colours	What's your favourite colour?
LESSON 15 Roundup	
LESSON 16 Whose sweater is this?	
Ask about and identify possessions	Whose sweater is this? It's Andy's. It isn't mine. It's hers.
LESSON 17 Who's your favourite star?	
Say who you like and who you don't like	I like him. I don't like her.
Give opinions	I think she's great! I think they're boring.
LESSON 18 Have you got a bike?	
Ask and talk about possessions	Have you got a bike? Yes, I have./No, I haven't. I've got a camera. I haven't got a watch.
LESSON 19 How many have you got?	
Ask and talk about collections	Have you got any 3D postcards? Yes, I have. I've got some posters. He hasn't got any stamps.
Ask and talk about quantity	How many has she got? She's got nearly 300.
LESSON 20 Roundup	
LESSON 21 How many are there?	
Ask and talk about statistics	How many students are there in Kate's class? There are thirty. How many people are there with brown hair? Are there any students with red hair? Yes, there are. No, there aren't.

LANGUAGE USE	LANGUAGE
LESSON 22 There's an attic.	
Ask and talk about rooms of a house	Is there an attic? Yes, there is. No, there isn't. There's a bedroom.
Ask and talk about location of rooms	Is there a kitchen on the ground floor?
LESSON 23 Spiders in the chimney.	
Ask and talk about furniture and furnishings	Is there a bed? Are there any chairs? There aren't any curtains.
Ask and talk about position	Where's the bed? It's next to the window. There's a box under the bed.
LESSON 24 I live in Dover.	
Ask and say where you live	Where do you live? I live in Dover.
Say where people live	My friend lives in Penzance.
Ask and say where places are	Where is Dover? It's in the south/on the south coast of England.
Describe places	There are many interesting places to see. Dover is famous for its chalk cliffs.
LESSON 25 Roundup	
LESSON 26 How do you spell it?	
Say the alphabet	A B C D etc.
Ask for spellings	How do you spell your surname?
Spell words	H-A-double R-I-S-O-N.
Ask and say what you want	Do you want a T-shirt or a poster? Can I have a T-shirt please?
LESSON 27 Can you swim under water?	
Ask and talk about abilities and physical skills	Can you speak English? Yes, I can./No, I can't. I can speak English.
Talk about degree of skill	She can't speak French very well.

LANGUAGE USE	LANGUAGE
LESSON 28 I'm doing my homework.	
Ask and say what you are doing	What are you doing? I'm doing my homework. Are you writing a postcard? Yes, I am./No, I'm not. You're writing a letter.
LESSON 29 She's wearing Number 13.	
Ask and say what people are doing	What is he/are they doing? She's/They're running. She isn't/They aren't diving.
Talk about order	They're second. He's last.
LESSON 30 Roundup	
LESSON 31 Do you like hamburgers?	
Ask and talk about likes and dislikes	Do you like hamburgers? Yes, I do./No, I don't.
Say what people like	Maria likes chips. She doesn't like milk.
Talk about tastes	I don't like onions. I don't like mustard, either.
Ask for food in a restaurant	Can I have some chips, please?
LESSON 32 Which ones do you like?	
Ask about and identify things you like	Which bag do you like? I like the pink one/that one. Which shorts do you like? I like the red ones/those. Do you like that sweater/these/those sweaters? Which one/ones?
Agree and disagree with people's tastes	Yes, I like it/them too.
Express approval	It's/They're really nice.
Offer assistance	Can I help you?
Refuse assistance in a shop politely	No, thanks. We're just looking.

LANGUAGE USE	LANGUAGE
LESSON 33 When have we got Maths?	
Ask and talk about your school timetable	When have we got Maths? On Monday. We've got Science on Friday afternoon.
Ask and talk about your best subjects	What are your best subjects? My best subjects are maths and science.
Exclaim	How horrible!
LESSON 34 Do you like swimming?	
Ask and talk about likes and dislikes	Do you like swimming? Yes, I do./No, I don't. I like playing tennis. I don't like swimming.
Compare likes and dislikes	So do I. Neither do I.
Compare skills	So can I. Neither can I.
Talk about people's likes and dislikes	George likes swimming but he doesn't like playing tennis.
LESSON 35 Roundup	
LESSON 36 A big golden Labrador.	
Ask about and describe animals	What's special about a giraffe? What's it like? It's got a long neck and large spots. It lives in Africa.
LESSON 37 It's too high!	
Ask and say what the matter is	What's the matter? It's too high!
Complain	Our school day is too long.
Give orders	Let go and drop!
LESSON 38 Speak loudly and clearly!	
Criticise the way people do things	You're speaking too quietly.
Instruct people to do things in a certain way	Speak loudly and clearly. Shut the door quietly.

LANGUAGE USE	LANGUAGE
LESSON 39 How tall is it?	
Ask and talk about measurement:	
height	How tall/high is it?
	It's 83.03 metres tall/high.
	How tall are you?
	I'm 1.55 metres tall.
length	How long is it?
	It's 260 metres long
width	How wide is it?
	It's 29 centimetres wide.
depth	How deep is it?
	It's 7 metres deep.
distance	How far is it from London to New York?
	Its 5,565 kilometres.

LESSON 40 Roundup

LANGUAGE USE	LANGUAGE
LESSON 41 How much are they?	
Ask and say the price of articles	How much are they?
	They're 20 pence each/a packet.
	That's 95p altogether.
Say what you want	I'd like a packet of crisps.
Ask about availability	Have you got any crisps?
	Have you got anything to eat?
Express hunger	I'm hungry.
Express thirst	I'm thirsty. I'd like something to drink.
Hurry people	Hurry up!
	It's time to go.

LANGUAGE USE	LANGUAGE
LESSON 42 What time is it?	
Ask and tell the time	What time is it?
	It's half past five.
Ask and talk about schedules	What time does the train leave?
	(It leaves) At eight o'clock.
Talk about routine	What time is supper?
	It's usually at seven.

LANGUAGE USE	LANGUAGE
LESSON 43 It's raining.	
Ask and talk about the weather	What's the weather like?
	It's raining.
	The sun's shining.
	It's very cold.
	It's raining.

LANGUAGE USE	LANGUAGE
LESSON 44 We have supper at seven.	
Ask and talk about domestic routine:	
times	What time do you get up?
	I get up at 7.45.
activities	What does she do after breakfast?
	She goes riding.
meals	What do they have for breakfast?
	They have bacon and eggs.

LESSON 45 Roundup

LANGUAGE USE	LANGUAGE
LESSON 46 What's 'goodbye' in Japanese?	
Ask and talk about words in a foreign language:	What's *goodbye* in Japanese?
	It's *sayonara*.
meaning	What does *sayonara* mean?
	It means *goodbye*.
spelling	How do you spell *sayonara*?
pronunciation	How do you pronounce *sayonara*?

LANGUAGE USE	LANGUAGE
LESSON 47 When's your birthday?	
Ask and talk about birthdays	When's your birthday?
	It's in July.
	It's on 4th September.
	It's in the summer.
Ask and talk about dates	What's the date today?
	It's 11th May.

LANGUAGE USE	LANGUAGE
LESSON 48 My sister never helps!	
Ask and talk about jobs in the home	Do you ever make your bed?
	Yes, always.
Say how often you do things	I never buy comics.
Say how often others do things	He always tidies his room.
	She sometimes does the washing up.
Ask and talk about spending	Do you ever buy sweets?
	I sometimes save my pocket money.

LANGUAGE USE	LANGUAGE
LESSON 49 Does she like chocolates?	
Ask and talk about likes and dislikes	Does she like fish?
	Yes, she does.
	No, she doesn't.
	She likes opera but she doesn't like ballet.
Ask for and make suggestions	What shall we get her?
	Let's get her a plant.

LESSON 50 Roundup

LESSON 1 Hello.

Hello. My name's Kate.

And my name's Andy. What's your name?

1 **Say hello and say your name.**

Hello. My name's ....

2 **Ask your friend's name.**

YOU: What's your name?
FRIEND: My name's ....

3 **Talk to another friend.**

YOU: Hello. My name's ....
What's your name?
FRIEND: My name's .... Hello.

Look!
my name's = my name is
what's = what is

4 **Listen and repeat.**

0 oh 1 one 2 two 3 three 4 four 5 five
6 six 7 seven 8 eight 9 nine 10 ten

Rhyme

Two and four and six and eight.
What's your name? My name is Kate.
One, three, five, seven, nine and ten.
Please, what is your name again?

LESSON 2 Good morning.

1 Say good morning or good afternoon to your teacher.

Good morning/afternoon, Miss/Mrs/Mr ....

2 Introduce yourself to a friend.

YOU: Hello. I'm ....
FRIEND: I'm .... Hello.

3 Imagine you are the people in the pictures. Introduce yourself.

Good morning. My name's Miss Harris. I'm Kate's teacher.

4 Copy and complete.

My name's Kate Morgan.   My .... Sue.
My brother's name is Andy.   My .... Miss Harris.

5 Write about you.

Write about:
   your name.
   your friend's name.   your mother's name.
   your teacher's name.   your father's name.

6 Say goodbye to some friends and to your teacher.

Look!
I'm = I am
my teacher's name = the name of my teacher

LESSON 3 — This is my family.

🔊 Dialogue

SUE: Hello, Mrs Morgan.
MRS MORGAN: Hello, Sue. How are you?
SUE: I'm OK, thanks.

KATE: Sue, this is my father.
Dad, this is Sue.
She's a friend from school.
SUE: Hello, Mr Morgan.
MR MORGAN: Hello, Sue.

KATE: And this is Andy.
He's my brother. We're twins.
SUE: I know Andy from school. Hello.
ANDY: Hi!

KATE: And this is Lucy.
She's my little sister.
LUCY: I'm a witch! Grr!
KATE: Go away, Lucy.
LUCY: No!
KATE: Yes!

1 Greet your friend.

YOU: Hello. How are you?
FRIEND: I'm OK, thanks. How are you?

2 🔊 Listen and repeat.

Sue is a friend from school.
She's a friend from school.

Andy is my brother.
He's my brother.

Andy and I are twins.
We're twins.

3 (three)

4 **Roleplay**

Work in groups. The others in your group are your family. Introduce your family to your teacher.

Mr Green, this is my mother.

5 Imagine you are Kate. Write about your family and friends. Start each sentence with **She's**, **He's**, or **We're**.

1. Lucy   She's . . . .
2. Andy
3. Andy and I
4. Mr Morgan
5. Mrs Morgan
6. Sue and I

6 Introduce two friends to each other.

YOU: Anna, this is Robert.
He's a friend from school.
ANNA: Hello, Robert.
ROBERT: Hello, Anna.

7 You have a famous friend. Introduce this famous friend to your teacher.

Miss Harris, this is my friend, Napoleon Bonaparte.

Look!
he's = he is
she's = she is
we're = we are

3 Talk about each person.

1. She's Kate's mother.

1. Mrs Morgan

2. Mr Morgan

3. Andy

4. Sue

5. John

6. Lucy

LESSON 4   He's called Big Ben.

📼 Dialogue

KATE: This is my cat.
SUE: What's her name?
KATE: Her name's Cleopatra but she's called Cleo.
SUE: Hello, Cleo.
ANDY: And this is our dog. His name's Benjamin but he's called Big Ben.
WOMAN: Sue! Sue! It's tea time.
KATE: Who's that?
SUE: That's my mum. I must go. Goodbye.
KATE: Bye.

1 Ask and answer about the people and pets below.

YOU: What's his name?
FRIEND: His name's Mr Morgan.
YOU: What's her name?
FRIEND: Her name's Miss Harris.

1. Mr Morgan
2. Miss Harris
3. Cleopatra
4. Mrs Morgan
5. Mr Green
6. Big Ben

5 (five)

1. PRINCE CHARLES
2. KING KONG
3. QUEEN ELIZABETH II
4. PRINCESS DIANA
5. TARZAN
6. STEVIE WONDER

2 Ask and answer about the people in the pictures.

YOU: What's his name?
FRIEND: That's Prince Charles.

3 Ask about the pictures again.

YOU: Who's that?
FRIEND: That's Prince Charles.

4 Show some photos of your family to your friend.

FRIEND: Who's that?
YOU: That's my little sister. Her name's Anna.

5 Say **goodbye** to a friend.

YOU: I must go. Goodbye.
FRIEND: Bye.

(six) 6

LESSON 5 Roundup

🔊 Conversation

Complete the conversation with Andy, Kate and Lucy.

ANDY: Hello. I'm Andy. What's your name?
YOU: My name's Mustyna
ANDY: This is my twin sister, Kate.
YOU: Hi
KATE: Hello.
ANDY: And this is my little sister, Lucy.
YOU: Hello Lucy
LUCY: Hello.
ANDY: And this is our dog.
YOU: What's his name
ANDY: Big Ben. And this is Kate's cat.
YOU: Wats her name
ANDY: Her name's Cleopatra. I must go. Goodbye.
YOU: Bay

Read

This is my family: my mother, my father, my brother Andy, my little sister Lucy and me. Andy and I are twins. We have a cat called Cleopatra and a dog called Big Ben.

This is my school. The name of my school is Castle Hill School. My teacher's name is Miss Harris. I have a friend at school. Her name is Sue.

Complete the sentences.

Andy is Kate's brother and Lucy is Kate and Andy's sister. Big Ben is the name of the family's dog and Cleopatra is the name of the family's cat. Miss Harris is Kate's teacher and Sue is Kate's friend.

Write

Write about your family and school.

Listen

Listen to the people. Who is speaking? Write the numbers of the pictures in the correct order.

1. 2
2. 3
3. 4
4. 1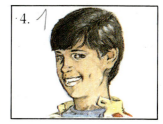

Quiz

Bring to class some photographs of some famous people. See if your friends know their names.

Grammar Lessons 1-5

Personal pronouns	Possessive adjectives	Verb 'to be' Present tense		
Singular	Singular	Singular		
I	my	I'm	=	I am
you	your	you're	=	you are
he	his	he's	=	he is
she	her	she's	=	she is
it	its	it's	=	it is
Plural	Plural	Plural		
we	our	we're	=	we are
you	your	you're	=	you are
they	their	they're	=	they are

| This is | my father. / our cat. | | Who's that? | | That's | Cleopatra. / my mum. |

| What's | your / his / her | name? |

| My / His / Her | name's | Kate. / Andy. / Lucy. |

| I / We | have a | cat. / friend. |

Her name's Cleopatra **but** she's called Cleo.

Andy is Kate's brother **and** Lucy is Kate's sister.

Definite article 'the'
the name of **the** school

Indefinite article 'a'
She's **a** friend.

Genitive apostrophe 's
Kate**'s** mother

Genitive with 'of'
The name **of** the school

LESSON 6 How old are you?

🔊 Dialogue

LUCY: I want to go on the Flying Octopus!
ANDY: No, Lucy. You're too young!
JOHN: How old are you, Lucy?
ANDY: She's only five.
JOHN: Are you only five, Lucy?
LUCY: No, I'm not. I'm nearly six!
ANDY: Let's go on the Dodgem Cars.
They're OK. Come on, Lucy.

1 🔊 Listen and repeat.

11 eleven   12 twelve   13 thirteen
14 fourteen   15 fifteen   16 sixteen
17 seventeen   18 eighteen
19 nineteen   20 twenty

2 Ask and answer the questions.

YOU: What's 2 + 9 (two and nine)?
FRIEND: 11 (eleven).

1. 2 + 5   3. 10 + 3   5. 1 + 19
2. 6 + 8   4. 7 + 12   6. 4 + 11

3 Count like this:

2, 4, 6 …
1, 3, 5 …
20, 19, 18 …

9 (nine)

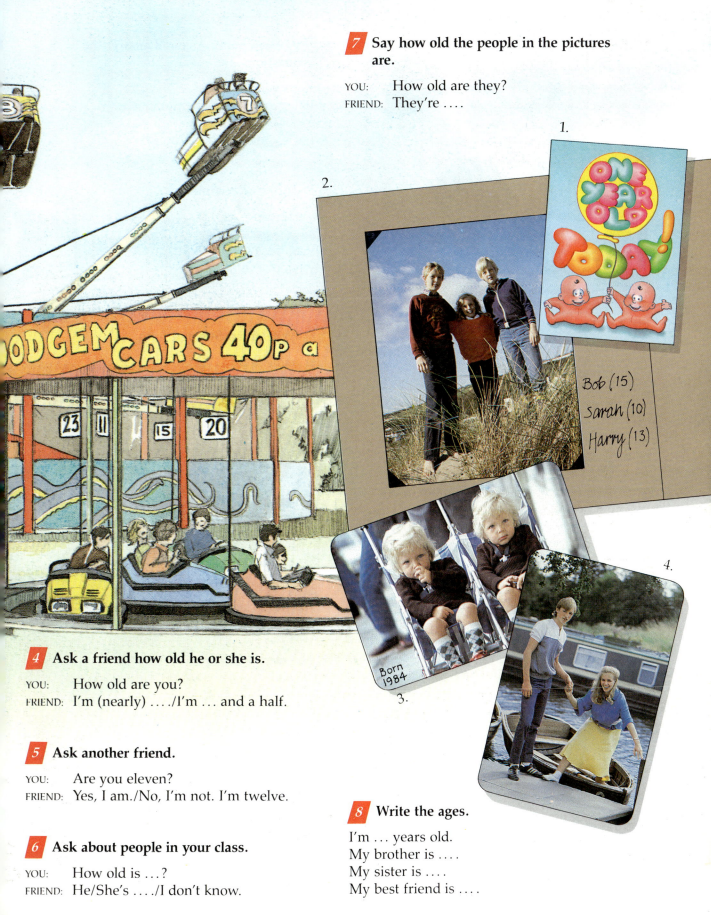

7 Say how old the people in the pictures are.

YOU: How old are they?
FRIEND: They're ....

Bob (15)
Sarah (10)
Harry (13)

Born 1984

4 Ask a friend how old he or she is.

YOU: How old are you?
FRIEND: I'm (nearly) ..../I'm ... and a half.

5 Ask another friend.

YOU: Are you eleven?
FRIEND: Yes, I am./No, I'm not. I'm twelve.

6 Ask about people in your class.

YOU: How old is ...?
FRIEND: He/She's ..../I don't know.

8 Write the ages.

I'm ... years old.
My brother is ....
My sister is ....
My best friend is ....

(ten) 10

LESSON 7 What's your address?

Dialogue

SUE: Look at my new address book! What's your address, Kate?
KATE: It's 65, Cliff Road, Dover.
SUE: And your telephone number?
KATE: It's 38872.
SUE: Say it again slowly.
KATE: Three — double eight — seven — two.
SUE: What's your favourite number?
KATE: Twenty-two. That's the number of our old house.

1 Listen and repeat.

20 twenty	30 thirty	40 forty	50 fifty
60 sixty	70 seventy	80 eighty	90 ninety
100 a hundred	23 twenty-three	37 thirty-seven	101 a hundred and one

2 Number buzz

Count round the class. After every four numbers the next person must say *buzz*.

1 2 3 4 BUZZ 6 7 8 9 BUZZ ...

3 Work in pairs. Ask and answer the questions.

What's your address?
What's your telephone number?
How old are you?
What's your favourite number?

4 Copy and complete.

My name is ...
I am ... years old.
My address is ...
My telephone number is ...
My favourite number is ...

5 Write about Sue and John.

Her name is Sue Wilson. She is ....

Name: Sue Wilson
Age: 12
Address: 41, Stratton Street, Dover
Telephone: Dover 50987

Name: John Dawson
Age: 12
Address: 32, Castle Street, Dover
Telephone: Dover 66221

6 Look it up!

```
Green S, 17 Blenheim Road, Dover ................ Dover 17902
Green S, 92 Albert Park Road, Dover ............. Dover 36149
Green S, 12 Queens Road, Dover .................. Dover 42691

Harris A W, 323 Manor Road, Dover ............... Dover 62271
Harris B, 12 Brook Road, Dover .................. Dover 57418
Harris B, 58 Chesterfield Drive, Dover .......... Dover 82790
```

Miss Harris's address is 12, Brook Road, Dover.
What's her telephone number?
Mr Green's telephone number is Dover 36149.
What's his address?

LESSON 8 What's this?

🔊 Dialogue

ANDY: Go away, Lucy.

LUCY: What's this?
ANDY: What?
LUCY: This. Is it a ruler?
ANDY: No, it isn't. It's a calculator.

LUCY: What's that?
ANDY: It's a cassette recorder. Now go away.

1 Ask and answer about the pictures below.

YOU: What's picture 1?
FRIEND: It's a ruler.

1. ruler
2. pencil
3. comic
4. pen
5. notebook
6. desk
7. stool
8. calculator
9. rubber
10. computer

2 Look again at the pictures in exercise 1. Ask and answer the questions.

Picture 1
YOU: What's this? Is it a ruler?
FRIEND: Yes, it is.

Picture 2
YOU: What's this? Is it a pen?
FRIEND: No, it isn't. It's a pencil.

1. a ruler?
2. a pen?
3. a comic?
4. a pencil?
5. a notebook?
6. a table?
7. a chair?
8. a computer?
9. a rubber?
10. a computer?

Look! What's **this**? What's **that**?

LESSON 9 It's an African elephant.

9

🔊 Dialogue

MR GREEN: Look at the picture on page thirty-five. Andy, what's this animal?
ANDY: It's an elephant.
MR GREEN: I know it's an elephant! But where is it from?
ANDY: India.
MR GREEN: No, you're wrong. It's from Africa. It's an African elephant. Look at its big ears. Now look at the next picture. What's this animal?
ANDY: I know. It's an Indian tiger.
MR GREEN: Good! Thank you, Andy.

Countries and nationalities

Africa	African
America	American
China	Chinese
England	English
India	Indian

1 Ask and say what the animals are.

YOU: What's this animal?
FRIEND: It's a bald eagle.

2 Ask and say what country the animals are from.

YOU: Where is it from?
FRIEND: It's from North America. It's an American bald eagle.

3 Draw or trace each animal and write about it.

This eagle is from North America.

> **Look!**
> a sheep dog   an elephant
> an English sheep dog   an African elephant

Did you know?

The elephant is the only animal with four knees.

(fourteen) 14

LESSON 10 Roundup

🔊 Conversation

Complete the conversation with Kate.

KATE: Hello. How are you?
YOU: ...I'm OK, ... And you
KATE: I'm fine thanks. Look at this. It's my new address book. What's your name?
YOU: My name is Mystem.
KATE: And your address?
YOU: Mielystowa 3B/59
KATE: How old are you?
YOU: I'm 15 years old.
KATE: I'm eleven. My brother Andy's eleven too. We're twins. Are you a twin?
YOU: No.
KATE: What's your favourite number?
YOU: My favorite number is 4
KATE: My favourite number is twenty-two. The number of our old house was twenty-two. I must go now. Bye!
YOU: Bye.

Read

This is Mr Green's class. Andy is one of Mr Green's students. Mr Green is a very good teacher. Andy has a pencil, a rubber and a book on his desk. Today the lesson is about wild animals. The picture of the African elephant is on page thirty-five of Andy's book. The elephant is nearly twelve years old.

Correct these statements.

1. Andy is a ~~teacher~~ student in Mr Green's class.
2. He has a pen, a pencil and a book on his desk.
3. The lesson is about ~~pets~~. Now
4. The animals are on page thirty-six of Andy's book.
5. The elephant is from ~~India~~. Now
6. The elephant is twelve years old. Nearly

Write

Write about your school. Copy and complete the sentences.

The name of my school is ....
My class is called Class ....
The name of my English teacher is ....
... is a ... good teacher.

10

 Listen

Listen and write the names of the animals in the order in which you hear them.

Project

Find out the names of:
- a big city in India.
- a wild animal from India.
- a country in Africa.
- a wild animal from Africa.
- a big city in China.
- a wild animal from China.

Grammar Lessons 6-10

How old	are	you? they?	I'm They're He's She's	twelve (years old).
	is	he? she?		

Are you eleven?

Yes, I am.
No, I'm not.

What's this/that?

It's	a ruler.
	an elephant.
	an Indian tiger.

Is it a ruler?

Yes, it is.
No, it isn't.

Where is it from?

It's from	Africa.
	India.
	England.

He She	has a book on	his her	desk.

Demonstrative pronoun
What's **this/that**?

Demonstrative adjective
What's **this/that** animal?

(sixteen) 16

LESSON 11 — He's American.

Dialogue

SUE: Who's that man?
ANDY: That's Harrison Ford.
SUE: Is he British?
ANDY: No, he isn't. He's American.

Countries and nationalities

Britain	British
France	French
Italy	Italian
Spain	Spanish
The United States of America (USA)	American

1 Ask and answer about the people in the pictures below.

YOU: Who's that woman?
FRIEND: That's Isabelle Huppert.
YOU: Where's she from?
FRIEND: She's from France.
YOU: Who's that man?
FRIEND: That's Severiano Ballesteros.
YOU: Where's he from?
FRIEND: He's from Spain.

1. ISABELLE HUPPERT (FRANCE)
2. SEVERIANO BALLESTEROS (SPAIN)
3. EDDIE MURPHY (USA)

2 Ask and answer about nationality.

YOU: Is he British?
FRIEND: No, he isn't. He's American.

YOU: Is she Italian?
FRIEND: Yes, she is.

Now ask about the people below:

1. French?   3. American?   5. Spanish?
2. Italian? 4. French?   6. British?

3 Ask and say what nationality you are.

YOU: What nationality are you?
FRIEND: I'm ....

4 Write about the men and women in the pictures.

1. The woman in picture one is Isabelle Huppert. She's French.
2. The man in picture two is ....

5 What is **hello** **and** thank you **in**:

French?
Spanish?
Chinese?

4. SOPHIA LOREN (ITALY)

5. HARRISON FORD (USA)

6. DALEY THOMPSON (BRITAIN)

LESSON 12 We're from Penzance.

🔊 Dialogue

BOY: Look out!
 Sorry!
KATE: That's OK. It doesn't matter.
 Are you English?
BOY: Yes, I am.
 This is my sister.
KATE: Hi. Where are you from?
GIRL: We're from Penzance.
ANDY: Where's that?
KATE: It's in Cornwall, silly!
MAN: Danny!
WOMAN: Linda!
KATE: Are they your parents?
BOY: No, they aren't.
 They're our uncle and aunt.
 OK, Aunt Alice.
 OK, Uncle Tom! We're coming.

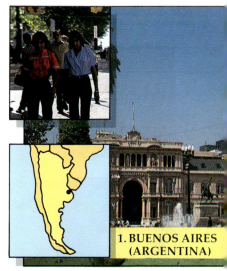

1. BUENOS AIRES (ARGENTINA)

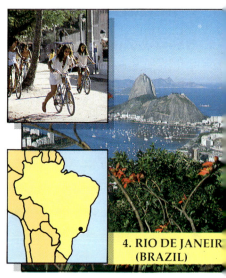

4. RIO DE JANEIR (BRAZIL)

Countries and nationalities

Argentina	Argentinian
Brazil	Brazilian
Germany	German
Greece	Greek
Japan	Japanese
Turkey	Turkish

1 Talk to the people in the pictures..

YOU: Where are you from?
FRIEND: We're from Buenos Aires.
YOU: Where's that?
FRIEND: It's in Argentina.

12

2. TOKYO (JAPAN)

3. ISTANBUL (TURKEY)

5. ATHENS (GREECE)

6. MUNICH (GERMANY)

2 Talk to the people again.

1. YOU: Are you Argentinian?
   FRIEND: Yes, we are.

2. YOU: Are you Chinese?
   FRIEND: No, we aren't. We're Japanese.

3. Turkish? 5. Greek?
4. French?   6. Spanish?

3 Write about the people.

The girls in picture one are from Buenos Aires in Argentina.
The boys ....
The children ....

4 Say what nationality you and your friends are, which town you are from and which country.

We're ....
We're from ..., in ....

Look!
1 boy — 2 boy**s**
1 girl — 2 girl**s**
1 child — 2 child**ren**
1 man — 2 m**e**n
1 woman — 2 wom**e**n

(twenty) 20

LESSON 13 Do you want a sweet?

🔊 Dialogue

KATE: Do you want a sweet?
GIRL: Yes, please.
KATE: Here you are.
GIRL: Thanks very much.
KATE: Do you want one?
BOY: What is it?
KATE: It's liquorice.
BOY: No, thanks. I hate liquorice.
GIRL: We must go now.
    Thanks for the sweet.
KATE: That's OK. Bye.

1 Offer and accept.

YOU: Do you want a.../some...?
FRIEND: Yes, please.
YOU: Here you are.
FRIEND: Thank you./Thanks.

a sweet

some sweets

a crisp

some crisps

a chocolate

some chocolates

an icecream

some chewing gum

2 Offer and refuse.

YOU: Do you want a.../some...?
FRIEND: No, thanks.

3 Offer and accept or refuse.

YOU: Do you want some liquorice?
FRIEND: Yes, please. I love liquorice./
    No, thanks. I hate liquorice.

4 Thank your friend for the icecream, the crisps and the chewing gum.

YOU: Thanks for the ....
FRIEND: That's OK.

5 Write and thank a friend for the following:

Thank you very much for the ....

21 (twenty-one)

LESSON 14 What colour are your eyes?

**What colour is your hair? What colour are your eyes?
What are your favourite colours?**

Name:	Kate	Lucy	Andy	John	Cleopatra
Hair:	black	blonde	black	dark brown	Its fur is black and white
Eyes:	brown	blue	brown	grey	light green
Favourite colours:	blue and bright pink	red and bright yellow	green and orange	blue and purple	

1 Ask and answer about the people.

YOU: What colour is Kate's hair?
FRIEND: It's black.
YOU: What colour are Kate's eyes?
FRIEND: They're brown.
YOU: What are her favourite colours?
FRIEND: They're blue and bright pink.

2 Write about each person.

Kate:
Her hair is black, her eyes are brown and her favourite colours are blue and bright pink.

3 Write about yourself.

My hair is ....

4 Think of someone in the class. Answer your partner's questions.

FRIEND: Is it a he or a she?/Is it a boy or a girl?
YOU: It's a he./It's a boy.
FRIEND: Is his hair black?
YOU: Yes, it is.
FRIEND: Are his eyes blue?
YOU: No, they aren't. They're brown.

5 Quiz

Write down the answers. You have one minute!
What colour is ... ?

a panda   *an apple*   *a cloud*

a tomato   *the sea*   *grass*

an elephant   *an orange*   *the sun*

a banana   *the sky*   *a tree*

Remember! Some can be more than one colour.

LESSON 15 Roundup

🔊 Conversation

Look at the information about Linda, then complete the conversation with her. Ask her questions.

Name: Linda (Lin) Haydon
Occupation: schoolgirl
Age: 13
Nationality: British
Home town: Penzance
Colour of hair: blonde
Colour of eyes: green
Favourite food: fish and chips

LINDA: Hello.
YOU: Hello. ....?
LINDA: Linda Haydon.
YOU: OK, Linda ...?
LINDA: I'm thirteen.
YOU: Are you schoolgirl
LINDA: Yes, I am.
YOU: ....?
LINDA: From Penzance, in Cornwall.
YOU: What's your favourite food
LINDA: Fish and chips.

Talk to your partner in the same way and make a chart.

Read

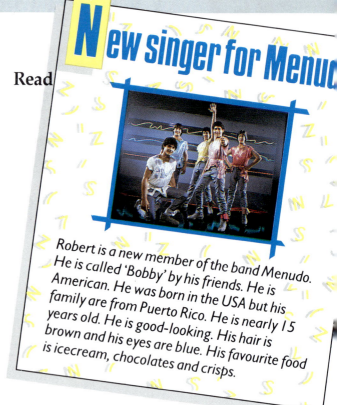

New singer for Menudo

Robert is a new member of the band Menudo. He is called 'Bobby' by his friends. He is American. He was born in the USA but his family are from Puerto Rico. He is nearly 15 years old. He is good-looking. His hair is brown and his eyes are blue. His favourite food is icecream, chocolates and crisps.

Answer the questions.

1. What is the boy called by his friends?
   a) Bob b) Robby c) Bobby

2. What nationality is he?
   a) British b) American c) Puerto Rican

3. Where are his family from?
   a) Puerto Rico b) The USA c) Britain

4. How old is he?
   a) fifteen b) sixteen c) fourteen

5. What colour are his hair and eyes?
   a) His hair is brown and his eyes are blue.
   b) They're brown.
   c) His hair is black and his eyes are blue.

6. What is his favourite food?
   a) chocolate crisps
   b) chocolate icecream and crisps
   c) chocolates, icecream and crisps

Write

Look at the information about Linda and the reading text about Robert. Write a paragraph about Linda.

Begin like this: Linda is a schoolgirl. She is called ....

15

🔊 Listen

Listen to the results of the British Grand Prix on the radio. Copy the chart on the right and complete it with the colour of the cars and the nationality of the drivers.

Project

Find out the countries where these cars come from:

| Citroen | Volkswagen | Jaguar | Buick |
| Seat | Alfa Romeo | Toyota | Volvo |

NAME	NATIONALITY	MODEL	COLOUR
Moreno	Italy	McLaren	~~Blue~~ Red
Gabon	France	Ferrari	Blu
Scott		Renault	Green
Marshall	American	Alfa Romeo	White

Grammar Lessons 11-15

Verb 'to be'
Singular

Am I				I am.			I'm not.
Are you	American?	Yes,	you are.	No,	you aren't.
Is he/she			he/she is.		he/she isn't.

Plural

	we				we				we	
Are	you	English?	Yes,	you	are.	No,	you	aren't.
	they				they				they	

	is	his	hair?	It's black.
What colour				
	are	her	eyes?	They're blue.

	love	sweets.			an orange?
I	hate	chewing gum.	Do you want	some	chewing gum?
					crisps?

Singular	*Plural*	*Singular*	*Plural*
a boy	some boys	a sweet	some sweets
a girl	some girls	a chocolate	some chocolates
a child	some children	a crisp	some crisps
a man	some men		
a woman	some women		

(twenty-four) 24

LESSON 16 Whose sweater is this?

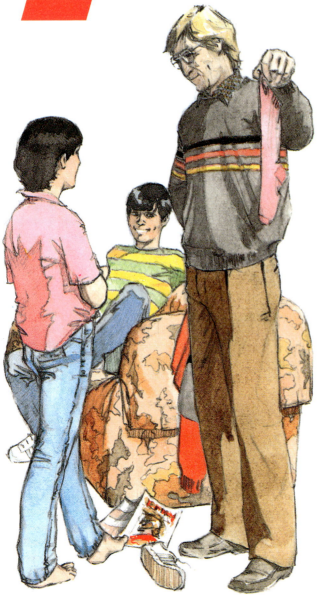

jeans

sweater

KATE'S CLOTHES

boots

T-shirt

anorak

trousers

 **Dialogue**

MR MORGAN: Kate, whose sweater is this?
Is it yours or Andy's?
KATE: It's Sue's.
MR MORGAN: Well, why is it here?
KATE: I don't know.
MR MORGAN: And whose socks are these?
Are these yours, Andy?
ANDY: Mine? Pink socks?
KATE: Well, they aren't mine.
ANDY: Perhaps they're yours, Dad.
MR MORGAN: Don't be cheeky!

MRS MORGAN'S CLOTHES

blouse

shoes

16

ANDY'S CLOTHES — trainers, socks

jacket, skirt

MR MORGAN'S CLOTHES — shirt

dress, coat

1 Look at the pictures. Ask and answer. Choose different clothes each time.

YOU: Whose sweater is this?
FRIEND: It's Andy's.
YOU: Whose boots are these?
FRIEND: They're Kate's.

Look!

| It's | my / your / his / her | sweater. | It's | mine. / yours. / his. / hers. |

2 Use the groups of clothes to complete the conversation.

MRS MORGAN: Is this Andy's T-shirt?
KATE: No, it isn't his. It's mine.
MRS MORGAN: Are these Kate's trainers?
ANDY: No, they aren't hers. They're mine.
MRS MORGAN: Are these Kate's jeans?
ANDY: ....
MRS MORGAN: Is this Andy's jacket?
KATE: ....
MRS MORGAN: Are these Andy's boots?
KATE: ....
MRS MORGAN: Is this Kate's sweater?
ANDY: ....
MRS MORGAN: Is this your dress, Kate?
KATE: ....
MRS MORGAN: Is this your blouse, Kate?
KATE: ....

3 Collect a few clothes and school things like pens and pencils. Hold up something and ask whose it is.

YOU: Whose jacket is this?
FRIEND: It's mine.

(twenty-six) 26

LESSON 17 # Who's your favourite star?

🎵 Dialogue

JOHN: Who's that?
SUE: That's Robert Power.
I think he's great.
Who's your favourite pop star?
JOHN: I don't know. I don't like
pop music much.
SUE: You are funny!
KATE: I like Bob Marley.
SUE: Yes, I like him too. And I also like
Tracey Ullman.
KATE: Oh, I don't like her. I think
she's horrible. Hey, is that a picture of
Wham!?
SUE: Yes, it is.
KATE: I like their new record.
SUE: I don't like it. I think it's boring.
JOHN: You're boring, you two. I'm going home.
See you!

Look!

I like Simon Le Bon. = I like **him**.
I don't like Tracey Ullman. = I don't like **her**.
I like Duran Duran. = I like **them**.
I don't like their record. = I don't like **it**.

1 Ask and answer.

YOU: Who's your favourite pop star or band?
FRIEND: I like ....
YOU: Yes, I like him/her/them too./
I don't like him/her/them.

2 Ask and answer.

FRIEND: What's your favourite record?
YOU: I like the new record by ....
FRIEND: Yes, I like it too./I don't like it.

3 Say what you think about famous people.

fantastic	horrible
great	boring
good	bad

I think David Bowie is fantastic.
I think their new record is bad.
I think they're great.

4 Copy and complete.

Favourite male pop star	
Favourite female pop star	
Favourite band	
Favourite record in the Top Ten	

Look at your friend's notes and compare them with yours.

5 Write about your favourites.

I like .... I think he/she's ....
I also like .... I think they're ....
My favourite record is ....

LESSON 18 Have you got a bike?

Dialogue

ANDY: Have you got a bike?
JOHN: Yes, I have. Have you?
ANDY: Yes, I've got a BMX.
JOHN: I've got one, too. What colour's yours?
ANDY: Mine's gold with black wheels. It's over there.
JOHN: Great! Let's see it.

1 Look at the pictures. Ask and answer about your possessions.

YOU: Have you got a bike?
FRIEND: Yes, I have. Have you?
YOU: No, I haven't./Yes, I have.

a bike
a camera
a watch
a tennis racket
a football
a stamp album
a radio
a tent
a pet
a sleeping bag

2 Talk about your possessions with a friend.

YOU: I've got a camera.
FRIEND: Yes, I've got one too./I haven't got one.

3 Write one sentence about some things you've got and one sentence about some things you haven't got.

I've got a watch, an old bike and a radio.
I haven't got a football or a tent.

4 Wordsearch

```
A C E F S H J L
R P W A T C H N
T X V Z A B D F
E A R E M A C I
K K M O P Q S T
I A D R A D I O
B N K H L Z Y U
F O O T B A L L
Q T U E U W Y R
C D S P M Z O M
```

Look at the word puzzle above and find the names of six other things from the pictures on the left. The words can go forwards (→) backwards (←) up (↑) or down (↓). You can use letters more than once.

Look!
I've = I have
I haven't = I have not

(twenty-eight) 28

LESSON 19 How many have you got?

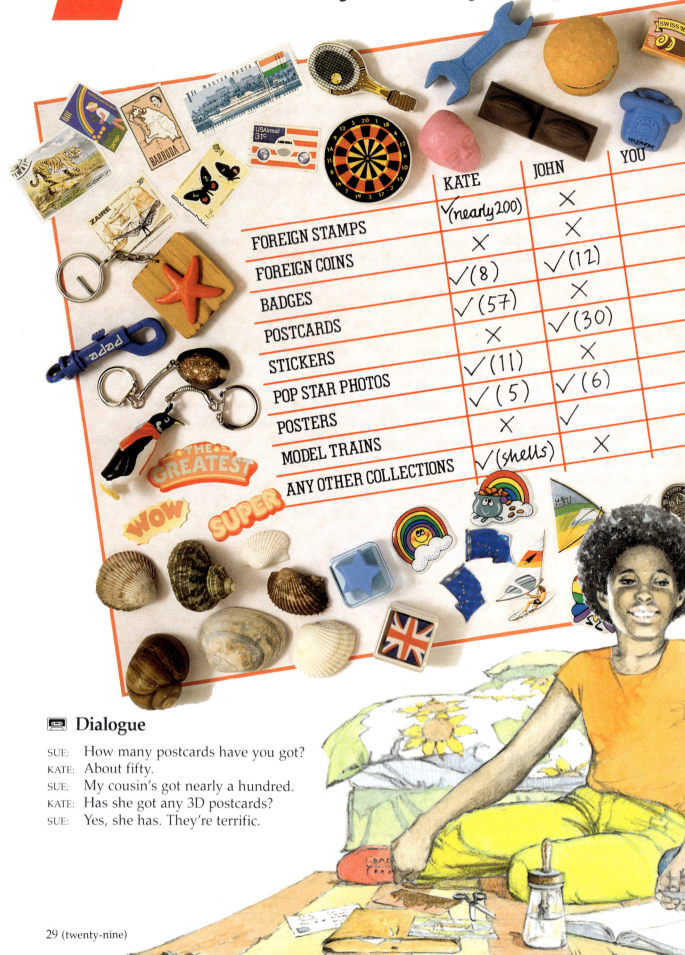

	KATE	JOHN	YOU
FOREIGN STAMPS	✓ (nearly 200)	✗	
FOREIGN COINS	✗	✗	
BADGES	✓ (8)	✓ (12)	
POSTCARDS	✓ (57)	✗	
STICKERS	✗	✓ (30)	
POP STAR PHOTOS	✓ (11)	✗	
POSTERS	✓ (5)	✓ (6)	
MODEL TRAINS	✗	✓	
ANY OTHER COLLECTIONS	✓ (shells)	✗	

Dialogue

SUE: How many postcards have you got?
KATE: About fifty.
SUE: My cousin's got nearly a hundred.
KATE: Has she got any 3D postcards?
SUE: Yes, she has. They're terrific.

19

1 Look at the chart of people's collections, put a tick (✓) for **yes** and the number of things in your collection, or put a cross (✗) for **no**.

Look!			
hasn't = has not			
I've	got		some postcards.
I haven't		any	postcards.
Have you			postcards?

2 Ask and answer about your collections.

YOU: Have you got any foreign stamps?
FRIEND: Yes, I have.
YOU: How many have you got?
FRIEND: Nearly three hundred.
YOU: Have you got any foreign coins?
FRIEND: No, I haven't.

3 Ask and answer about Kate and John.

YOU: Has Kate got any foreign stamps?
FRIEND: Yes, she has. She's got nearly two hundred.
YOU: Has she got any foreign coins?
FRIEND: No, she hasn't.

4 Write about collections.

Kate's got some stamps, some badges, some postcards, some photos of pop stars, some posters and some shells. She hasn't got any foreign coins, stickers or model trains.

John's got ...
My friend's got ...
I've got ...

5 Picture puzzle

Take the first letter of each of the following and see what Andy collects.

1. 2. 3. 4.
5. 6.

(thirty) 30

LESSON 20 Roundup

🔊 Conversation

Complete the conversation with Andy.

ANDY: Hello.
YOU: *Hello*
ANDY: How are you?
YOU: *OK.*
ANDY: Do you know, I've got three uncles, two aunts and ten cousins. What about you?
YOU: *1 uncels, 1 aunts, 2 cousins*
ANDY: Who's your favourite pop band?
YOU: *Whitney Houston*
ANDY: Yes, I like them too. I think they're great. And I like Michael Jackson.
YOU: *I dont like*
ANDY: Have you got any collections?
YOU: *No I'm not*
ANDY: I've got six wild life posters. Well, I'm going home now. Bye!
YOU: *Bye*

🔊 Listen

Listen to Jessica. Write the numbers of the topics below in the order in which she talks about them.

1. Her pets *2*
2. Her family *1*
3. Her collections *5*
4. Her favourite clothes *3*
5. Her opinion of Michael Jackson *4*

Read

His name is Michael Jackson — super- super-super-star! Have you got any Michael Jackson songs? Perhaps you've got one of his hit albums or videos. Millions of people all over the world like Michael Jackson.

Michael has got three sisters and five brothers. The boys are all in the band called The Jackson Five, but Michael is the international superstar. Why do people like him? They like his music, they like his songs and they like his dancing. They even like his clothes: his boots covered with sequins, the silver glove on his left hand, and his blue and gold sequinned jacket and black trousers.

On stage Michael is a star but at home he is quiet and shy. He lives in a very big house in Encino, California with his mother, Katherine, and two of his sisters, Janet and La Toya. He loves animals. He's got lots of animals in his private zoo, including an eight-foot long boa constrictor snake called Muscles and a sheep called Mr Tibbs.

Michael Jackson quiz

1. Who are The Jackson Five?
2. How many sisters has Michael Jackson got?
3. Who is Katharine?
4. Who are Janet and La Toya?
5. Where are Michael Jackson's animals?
6. What is Muscles?
7. What is Mr Tibbs?

Write

Write sentences about your family. Say how many brothers and sisters you've got and what their names are.

Write about your collections or pets. Say what they are.

Write about your favourite clothes and what colour they are.

Write about your favourite pop stars and music.

Swap Shop

Make a list of things you have got but you don't want. Then make another list of things you want but you haven't got. With your friends, see how many things you can swap, like this:

'Who wants to swap … for … ?'

Grammar Lessons 16-20

Possessive pronouns	Object pronouns
mine	me
yours	you
his	him
hers	her
its	it
ours	us
theirs	them

Whose	sweater is this?	It's mine.
	socks are these?	They're his.

Have you	got	a camera?
Has he/she		any stamps?

Yes,	I	have.
No,		haven't.

Yes,	he/she	has.
No,		hasn't.

I've	got	a camera.
I haven't		one.

I've got some	stamps.
I haven't got any	

I	like	Tracey Ullman.
		Simon Le Bon.
	don't like	Duran Duran.
		their new record.

I think	she's	great.
	he's	boring.
	they're	good.
	it's	bad.

LESSON 21 How many are there?

🎧 Dialogue

KATE: Guess what!
ANDY: What?
KATE: There are twenty-two people with brown hair in my class.
ANDY: That's a lot. How many are there in your class altogether?
KATE: Only thirty!

1 Look at the class record book. Ask and answer about Kate's class.

How many students are there in Kate's class altogether?
There are ... students.
　　　　 ... girls.
　　　　 ... boys.

2 Ask and answer about your class.

33 (thirty-three)

CASTLE HILL SCHOOL

Class: 1A
Total number of students: 30
Number of girls: 17
Number of boys: 13

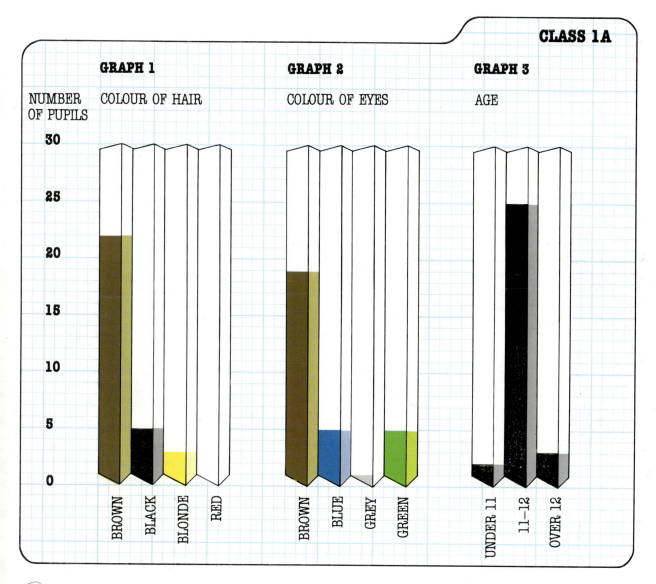

 Ask and answer questions from the graphs.

Graph 1
YOU: How many students are there with brown hair?
FRIEND: There are twenty-two.

Graph 2
YOU: How many students are there with brown eyes?
FRIEND: There are nineteen.

Graph 3
YOU: How many students are there under eleven years old?
FRIEND: There are . . . .

 Ask and answer more questions.

Graph 1
YOU: Are there any students with brown hair?
FRIEND: Yes, there are.
YOU: Are there any students with red hair?
FRIEND: No, there aren't.

 Make your own class graphs and write about them.

Hair: In my class there are . . . students with . . . hair, . . . with . . . hair and . . . .

Eyes: There are . . . .

Age: There are . . . .

(thirty-four) 34

LESSON 22 — # There's an attic.

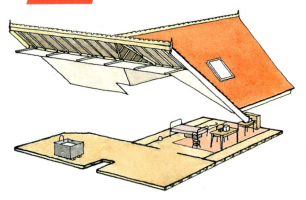

2 Ask and answer about the rooms.

YOU: Is there a kitchen on the ground floor?
FRIEND: Yes, there is.

YOU: Is there a kitchen on the next floor?
FRIEND: No, there isn't

1. kitchen
2. play room
3. sitting room
4. bedroom
5. dining room
6. toilet
7. bathroom

3 In pairs, ask each other about rooms in your homes.

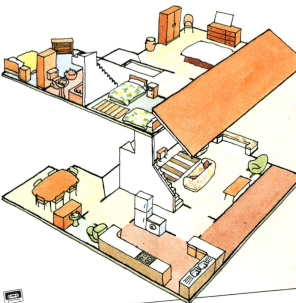

Our house

Our house is quite big. There are two floors and an attic. Downstairs on the ground floor there is a sitting room, a dining room, a kitchen and a toilet. Upstairs on the next floor there is a bathroom and three bedrooms. The big bedroom is my parents' room. Kate and Lucy's room is opposite theirs. My bedroom is the small one. Our play room is in the attic in the roof. That's the best room in the house.

1 Read and answer.

1. How many rooms are there downstairs?
2. How many bedrooms are there upstairs?
3. Whose is the big bedroom?
4. Where is Kate and Lucy's bedroom?
5. Whose is the small bedroom?
6. Where is the play room?

4 Where am I?

You are in one of the rooms of the house. Write down the name of the room and give it to your teacher. Your friends must guess where you are.

FRIEND 1: Are you in the bathroom?
YOU: No, I'm not.
FRIEND 2: Are you in the big bedroom?

Look!

my parents' room = the room of my parents.

LESSON 23 Spiders in the chimney.

The attic is our favourite room. It's at the top of the house. There are some stairs up to it and a very small door. There's a notice on the door saying 'PRIVATE'.

The attic is dark and a bit spooky. Lucy's afraid of it but I'm not. I like it because it's ~~ourts~~ ours.

There are lots of things in it. There's an old bed next to the wall. There's a desk, a big table and some chairs next to the window. There are some spiders and a bird's nest in the chimney.

In the corner there's an enormous cupboard. It's full of games, old toys, dolls and clothes.

On the walls there are lots of flags, and posters, and some photos of pop stars and my favourite football team. There's also a picture of Big Ben by Lucy. (It's ~~horribe~~ horrible.)

There aren't any curtains but there's an old red carpet on the floor. Under the bed there's a big black box with a lock for my models and badges.

I like the attic best when I'm alone in it.

* * * * * * * * * *

1 True or False?

1. The attic has got a very big door.
2. Lucy likes the attic.
3. There are lots of things in the attic.
4. There is a bed next to the window.
5. There are some chairs in the room.
6. There aren't any posters on the wall.
7. There is a picture of Cleopatra.
8. There aren't any curtains.
9. There is a big black box in the cupboard.

2 Answer these questions about the attic. Use:

Yes, there is.	No, there isn't.
Yes, there are.	No, there aren't.

Is there a bed in the room?
    a typewriter on the bed?
    a carpet on the floor?
    a box under the table?
    a bird's nest in the chimney?
Are there any curtains?
    any chairs?
    any models on the table?
    any spiders on the bed?
    any posters on the walls?

3 Say where everything is. Answer these questions. Use:

in   next to
on   under

Where is the bed?
    the bird's nest?
    the cupboard?
    the typewriter?
    the carpet?
    the box?
    the notice saying 'PRIVATE'?
Where are the table and chairs?
    the posters?
    Andy's models?

Rhyme

I know a house
It's a nice old house.
It's a nice old house
In a square.
And in that house
There's a funny old ghost
And he's just behind
Your chair.
Aaagh!

LESSON 24   **I live in Dover.**

Kate is writing a letter to her new penfriend. Her name is Rachel Jones and she lives in Australia.

65, Cliff Rd,
Dover,
Kent
23rd November

Dear Rachel,

My name is Kate Morgan. I'm eleven years old and I live in Dover. (That's on the south-east coast of England.). I am in class 1A at Castle Hill School. My twin brother, Andy, goes to the same school but he's in a different class.

South-east England

DOVER
THE GATEWAY TO EUROPE

1 Read and answer.

1. Where is Dover?
2. Why is it important?
3. What is Dover sometimes called?
4. Is the port busy?
5. Are there any Roman remains in Dover?
6. Where's the castle?
7. Where are the gardens?
8. What else is Dover famous for?

Dover is a large town in the south-east of England. It is a big, busy port and an important link between Britain and Europe. Dover is sometimes called the 'gateway to Europe'. Car ferries, hovercraft and boats go in and out of the port every day.

There are many interesting places to see in Dover. There is a Roman lighthouse, and the remains of a Roman house. There is also an old castle on top of Castle Hill. If you like flowers and trees, there are some very beautiful gardens in the centre of the town. Dover is also famous for its chalk cliffs – the famous 'White Cliffs of Dover'.

2 Look at this map of Britain. Say where the towns are.

Southampton is in the south/on the south coast of England.

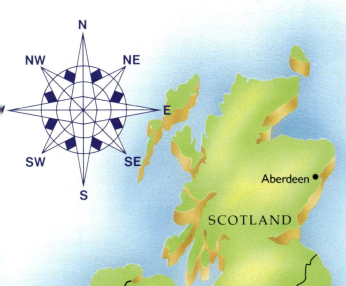

3 Look at the notes about Dover and write similar information about two large towns in your country.

NAME OF TOWN	Dover
SITUATION	south-east of England
PLACES TO SEE	the 'White Cliffs of Dover' a castle some gardens
HISTORICAL REMAINS	a Roman lighthouse the remains of a Roman house

4 Write a few sentences about the two towns.

... is a large town in .... There are many interesting places to .... There is .... There are also some/many ....

5 Ask and answer.

YOU: Where do you live?
FRIEND: I live in the centre of ..... That's in the north of .... I live near ....

6 Write about your friend.

My friend lives in ....

Look!
in the north of England
on the south coast of Britain
in the centre of London

🎧 **Rhyme**

In the north, in the south, in the east, in the west,
Wherever you live, your home is the best.

(thirty-eight) 38

LESSON 25 Roundup

Read

Read the description of the house, trace the diagram and then complete it.

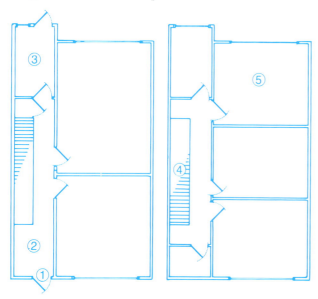

Ground floor
① Front door
② Hall
③ Kitchen

First floor
④ Stairs
⑤ Play room

This house is quite big. There are two floors. Downstairs there's a sitting-room on the right, and next to the sitting-room is a dining room. There's a kitchen opposite the front door, next to the dining room. There's a small toilet under the stairs. Upstairs there are three bedrooms, a play room and a bathroom. Two of the bedrooms are quite big. The small bedroom is over the kitchen and the bathroom is at the top of the stairs, over the hall.

Listen

Listen to this radio advertisement
Write down the rooms the person describes.

Write

Write a few sentences describing:

1. Your house/flat and your bedroom.
2. Your school and your classroom.

Begin like this:
Our flat is quite small. There are ....

Conversation

Complete the conversation with Kate.

KATE: Hello. How are you?
YOU: ....
KATE: Guess what! There are only four people with blonde hair in my class.
How many are there in your class?
YOU: ....
KATE: How many people are there in your class altogether?
YOU: ....
KATE: How many boys and how many girls?
YOU: ....
KATE: There are lots of posters and pictures on the wall in our classroom, and a map of Dover. What have you got on your classroom walls?
YOU: ....
KATE: I know a joke about spiders. What's black, hairy and horrible, with eight legs, and says 'ting-a-ling-a-ling!'?
YOU: ....
KATE: A spider on a bicycle!

Project

Are there too many people in the world?
Complete the chart for this year.

| WORLD POPULATION IN MILLIONS ||||
COUNTRY	1960	1981	THIS YEAR
CHINA	668	1,029	
INDIA	435	750	
EUROPE	425	490	
USSR	214	275	
USA	181	236	
BRAZIL	73	133	
YOUR COUNTRY			

Joke time!

CUSTOMER: Waiter! Waiter! There are six spiders in my soup.
WAITER: I know. It's their bath night!

Guessing game

There is a horrible spider somewhere in the room. Think of a place and write it down. The others must guess where it is.

Is it in the chimney?
Is it on the wall?

Grammar Lessons 21-25

| How many children are there? | There are forty-five. |

Is	there	a desk	in your room?
Are		any chairs	

Yes,		is.
No,	there	isn't.
Yes,		are.
No,		aren't.

	's	an	old	castle in my town.	
There	are	some / many	beautiful / interesting	gardens / things to see	in Dover.
	aren't	any			

| Where's the box? | It's | in / under / on / next to / near | the bed. |

| Where's (name of place)? | It's | in the | north / south / east / west / centre | of Britain. |

| It's on the | north / south / east / west | coast of Britain. |

| I live / He/she lives | in | Dover. / the centre of Belfast. / the north of England. |

| Why is Dover important? | Because it's a link between Britain and Europe. |

Possessive adjective
its

Possessive pronouns
ours
theirs

Genitive plural
my parents' room

LESSON 26 How do you spell it?

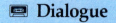 Dialogue

MAN: T-shirts and posters with your name on!
SUE: Come and have a look Kate.
MAN: Do you want a T-shirt or a poster?
SUE: Can I have a T-shirt, please?
MAN: OK. What's your name?
SUE: Sue Wilson.
MAN: How do you spell your surname?
SUE: W-I-L-S-O-N.
MAN: Do you want anything else on it?
SUE: Yes. I want 'Sue Wilson is great, OK?'

The alphabet
There are twenty-six letters in the English alphabet:

A B C D E F G H I J K L M N O P Q R S T U V W X Y Z
a b c d e f g h i j k l m n o p q r s t u v w x y z

There are five vowels:

A E I O U

and twenty-one consonants:

B C D F G H J K L M N P Q R S T V W X Y Z

1  Listen and repeat.

2 Ask and answer about names.

YOU: What's your surname?
FRIEND: Harrison.
YOU: How do you spell it?
FRIEND: H-A- double R-I-S-O-N.

3 Spelling quiz

How do you spell it in English?

1. The name of your country
2. The name of your capital city
3. The name of your school
4. The name of your headmaster or headmistress
5. The capital of France
6. The capital of Brazil
7. The capital of Japan
8. The president of the United States

41 (forty-one)

4 It is your birthday. Look at the pictures below and say what you want.

FRIEND: Do you want a torch or a bicycle lamp?
YOU: Can I have a torch, please?

a torch   a bicycle lamp

a record   a cassette

a wallet   a purse   a pair of scissors   a penknife

a comb   a brush   some jeans   some trainers

Joke time!

Mississippi is a big word. How do you spell it?
M.I.S.S...
No, you're wrong. The answer is 'I.T.'

LESSON 27 Can you swim under water?

THE CHAMPIONS

Can you run fast?
Can you climb a rope?
Can you swim under water?

You can? That's terrific!
Do you want to be a member of the Dover Team for
The Champions Competition?

You do? That's great!
Please send your name, address, age,
the name of your school and the name of your sports teacher to:
The Champions Competition, Room 6, The Town Hall, Dover.

27

1 Look at the chart and answer the questions about you. Write Yes, No, or Not very well.

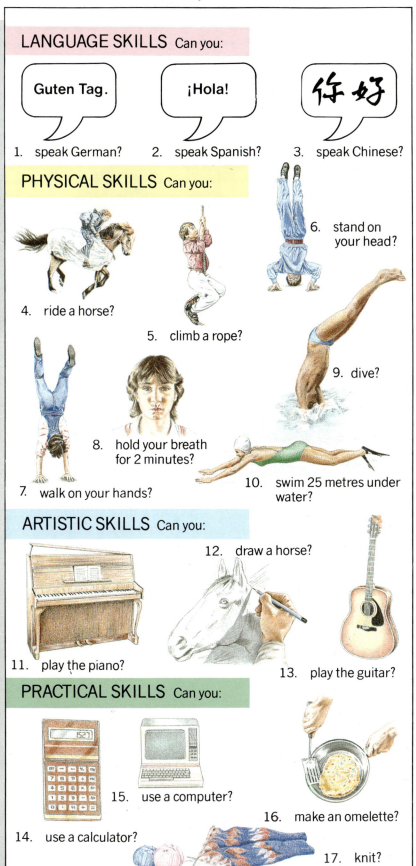

LANGUAGE SKILLS Can you:
1. speak German? (Guten Tag.)
2. speak Spanish? (¡Hola!)
3. speak Chinese? (你好)

PHYSICAL SKILLS Can you:
4. ride a horse?
5. climb a rope?
6. stand on your head?
7. walk on your hands?
8. hold your breath for 2 minutes?
9. dive?
10. swim 25 metres under water?

ARTISTIC SKILLS Can you:
11. play the piano?
12. draw a horse?
13. play the guitar?

PRACTICAL SKILLS Can you:
14. use a calculator?
15. use a computer?
16. make an omelette?
17. knit?

2 Work in pairs. Ask and answer the questions and write Yes, No or Not very well for your friend.

YOU: Can you speak German?
FRIEND: Yes, I can but not very well. Can you?
YOU: No, I can't.

Look!
can't = cannot

3 Tell your teacher what your friend can and cannot do.

Marianne can speak German but she can't speak English very well.

4 From each section of the chart, write sentences about some of the things you can do and some of the things you cannot do.

I can play the piano but I can't play the guitar.

Did you know?

Llamas can move their ears one at a time or both together.

(forty-four) 44

LESSON 28 I'm doing my homework.

🎧 Dialogue

LUCY: What are you doing?
ANDY: Go away. I'm doing my homework.
LUCY: No, you aren't. You're writing a letter.
ANDY: No, I'm not.
LUCY: Yes, you are! You're writing to Amanda. Is she your girlfriend?
ANDY: Be quiet and mind your own business!
LUCY: Andy's got a girlfriend! Andy's got a girlfriend!

1 Ask the people in the pictures below what they're doing. Imagine you are the people.

YOU: What are you doing, Andy?
FRIEND: I'm writing a letter.

1. *writing a letter*   2. *playing with a spelling game*

3. *listening to the radio*   4. *watching TV*

5. *talking to a friend on the telephone*   6. *making some toffee*

2 Talk to the people in the pictures again.

YOU: Are you writing a postcard, Andy?
FRIEND: No, I'm not. I'm writing a letter.
YOU: Are you playing with a spelling game, Lucy?
FRIEND: Yes, I am.

1. Andy   writing a postcard?
2. Lucy   playing with a spelling game?
3. Kate   listening to a cassette?
4. Mrs Morgan   watching TV?
5. Mr Morgan   talking to your mother?
6. John   making some hot chocolate?

3 Mime an action (swimming, walking, etc) and see if your friends can guess what you're doing.

Look!

| do | do**ing** | write | writ**ing** |
| talk | talk**ing** | make | mak**ing** |

LESSON **29** She's wearing Number 13.

1. Alan Wells
200 metres

2. Poland v Italy
football

3. Brazil v Yugoslavia volleyball

4. Marita Koch
200 metres

5. Michael Gross
100 metres butterfly

1 Ask and say what the people in the pictures above are doing.

YOU: What is he doing in picture 1?
FRIEND: He's running.

YOU: What are they doing in picture 2?
FRIEND: They're playing football.

2 Correct the statements about the pictures above.

1. He's running in the 800 metres.
He isn't running in the 800 metres, he's running in the 200 metres.
2. They're playing basketball.
They aren't playing basketball, they're playing football.

1. He's running in the 800 metres.
2. They're playing basketball.
3. Brazil are playing Germany.
4. She's running in the Marathon.
5. He's diving.

Dialogue

JOHN: I can see Tracy. She's wearing Number 13.
SUE: That's unlucky.
JOHN: She's standing next to Mrs Todd.
SUE: That's unlucky, too!
JOHN: What are Tracy and Simon doing? I don't understand.
SUE: They're tying a scarf round their ankles. It's the three-legged race!
MAN: On your marks, get set, go!
JOHN: Can you see them? Are they first?
SUE: No, they aren't. They're third.
JOHN: Sit down, Sue. I can't see!
SUE: No. You stand up instead. Look, they're second now.
KATE: Come on Dover!

Look!
first
second
third
last

(forty-six) 46

LESSON 30 Roundup

Listen and read

Correct these statements.

1. Nicola and Jack are at school.
   No, they aren't. They're on holiday.

1. Nicola and Jack are at school.
2. They are swimming on Puffin Island.
3. The men are wearing sweaters and jeans.
4. The men are rowing to the beach.
5. Jack and Nicola are having a cup of tea.
6. Jack and Nicola are fishing on the island.

Conversation

Complete the conversation with Andy.

ANDY: How do you spell your surname?
YOU: ....
ANDY: OK. What sports and games are you doing at school now?
YOU: ....
ANDY: What languages are you learning?
YOU: ....
ANDY: Can you speak French?
YOU: ....
ANDY: I can speak a little but not very well. I must go now. Bye!
YOU: ....

Write

Look again at the picture story and write sentences to say what is happening in the pictures.

Nicola and Jack are watching ...

Did you know?

The giant tortoises of the Galapagos Islands can live over 150 years.

Grammar Lessons 26-30

| How do you spell | your surname? / it? | S-M-I-T-H. |

What	are	you / they	doing?	I'm / We're / They're / He/She's	writing a letter.
	is	he/she			

Are	you / they	writing a letter?	Yes,	I am. / we are. / they are. / he/she is.	No,	I'm not. / we / they	aren't.
Is	he/she					he/she	isn't.

| I'm not / He/She isn't / They aren't | reading a comic. |

| Can | you / he/she | swim? | Yes, | I / he/she | can. | No, | I / he/she | can't. |

| I / He/She | can | swim (but not very well). / speak French (well). | I / He/She | can't speak Spanish (very well). |

| Do you want a T-shirt or a poster? | Can I have a T-shirt please? |

LESSON 31 Do you like hamburgers?

📼 Dialogue

MAN: Next, please.
MR MORGAN: What do you want, Kate?
KATE: Can I have a cheeseburger and chips, please?
MR MORGAN: Two cheeseburgers and chips, please.
MAN: Do you want them with or without onions?
KATE: Without.
MR MORGAN: She doesn't like onions.
MAN: Do you want mustard?
KATE: No thanks. I don't like mustard, either. Just ketchup, please.

1 Look at the menu and find:

a cheeseburger   a milkshake
a hamburger   a cup of coffee
chips   an orange juice
apple pie   a Pepsi Cola

49 (forty-nine)

FOOD

tomato soup

fish and chips

chicken

apple pie

THINGS TO GO WITH FOOD

salt and pepper   mustard   tomato ketchup   onions

DRINKS

coffee   milk   tea   Coca-Cola

orange juice   chocolate milkshake   banana milkshake   strawberry milkshake

2 Ask and answer.

YOU: Do you like tomato soup?
FRIEND: Yes, I do.
YOU: Do you like fish and chips?
FRIEND: No, I don't.

3 Write down all the things you like and all the things you don't like. Write two lists: I like ... I don't like ...

4 Change lists with your partner and write two things your partner likes and two things your partner doesn't like.

Maria likes hamburgers and chips but she doesn't like tomato ketchup or onions.

Did you know?

The biggest hamburger ever made was in Perth, Australia in 1976. It weighed 1,297 kilograms and measured 8.38 metres round!

(fifty) 50

LESSON 32 — # Which ones do you like?

🔊 Dialogue

MR MORGAN: Which trainers do you like? Do you like those?
KATE: Which ones?
MR MORGAN: The grey ones.
KATE: No, I don't. I like the pink ones. They're really nice.
WOMAN: Can I help you?
KATE: No, thanks. We're just looking at trainers.
WOMAN: Fine. Our new trainers are in the window.

1 Choose and point to the ones you like.

YOU: Which sports bag do you like?
FRIEND: I like that/this one.
YOU: Which trainers do you like?
FRIEND: I like these/those.

1. sports bags   2. trainers

3. shorts   4. sweaters

5. T-shirts   6. anoraks

 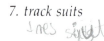

7. track suits   8. roller skates

2 Say what you like.

YOU: I like the red and silver sports bag.
FRIEND: I don't. I like the green one./Yes, I like it too. It's really nice.

YOU: I like the blue trainers.
FRIEND: I don't. I like the red ones./Yes, I like them too. They're really nice.

3 Ask and answer.

YOU: Do you like these/those shorts?
FRIEND: Which ones?
YOU: The white ones.
FRIEND: Yes, I do./No, I don't.

4 Look at the items in exercise 1 again and write five sentences about the things you like and don't like.

I like the blue trainers but I don't like the red ones.

5 Write down two things your partner likes and two things your partner doesn't like.

Tony likes the green sports bag but he doesn't like the red and silver one. He likes....

LESSON 33 — When have we got Maths?

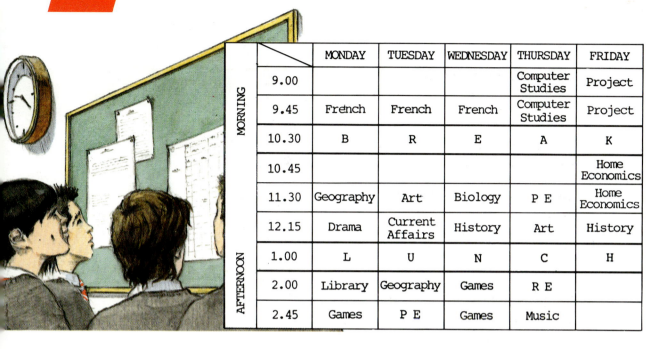

		MONDAY	TUESDAY	WEDNESDAY	THURSDAY	FRIDAY
MORNING	9.00				Computer Studies	Project
	9.45	French	French	French	Computer Studies	Project
	10.30	B	R	E	A	K
	10.45					Home Economics
	11.30	Geography	Art	Biology	P E	Home Economics
	12.15	Drama	Current Affairs	History	Art	History
AFTERNOON	1.00	L	U	N	C	H
	2.00	Library	Geography	Games	R E	
	2.45	Games	P E	Games	Music	

📼 Dialogue

ANDY: Oh no! We've got English on Monday, Tuesday and Wednesday morning.
JOHN: When have we got Maths?
ANDY: Every day except Friday. And look! We've got double Science with Mr Bragg.
JOHN: When?
ANDY: On Friday afternoon.
JOHN: How horrible!

1 Read the dialogue and complete the timetable above.

2 On which day or days is:

1. Biology?
   It's on Wednesday.

1. Biology?
2. History?
3. Computer Studies?
4. French?
5. Games?
6. Home Economics?

3 Ask and say exactly when the lessons are.

YOU: When is Biology?
FRIEND: It's on Wednesday morning.

4 Talk about your timetable.

YOU: When have we got Games?
FRIEND: On Monday and Wednesday afternoon.

5 Ask and answer.

YOU: What are your best subjects?
FRIEND: My best subjects are Maths and Science. What are yours?

6 📼 Listen, and repeat.

The days of the week:
Monday   Friday
Tuesday   Saturday ⎫
Wednesday   Sunday   ⎬ the weekend
Thursday

📼 Rhyme

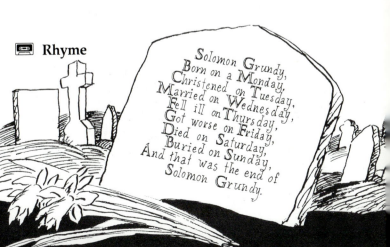

Solomon Grundy,
Born on a Monday,
Christened on Tuesday,
Married on Wednesday,
Fell ill on Thursday,
Got worse on Friday,
Died on Saturday,
Buried on Sunday,
And that was the end of
Solomon Grundy.

LESSON 34 Do you like swimming?

What do you like doing in your free time? Do you like swimming, riding and sailing? You do? Then come and join us here at Camp Sherwood. It's the perfect place for an adventure holiday.
Look at the questionnaire. Tick the things that you like doing and put a star by the activities that you can do well. Send the form to Barry Smith at the following address: Camp Sherwood, PO Box 12, Taunton, Somerset

Outdoor activities

Do you like:
horse riding?
riding BMX bikes?
climbing?
birdwatching?
playing tennis?
playing football?

1 Look at the brochure above. Write down your two favourite activities from each group. Then write a sentence about each activity.

I like playing tennis very much.

Look!
So do I.   Neither do I.
So can I. Neither can I.

2 Write down an activity from each group that you don't like doing very much. Then write a sentence about each activity.

I don't like playing football very much.

3 Talk about the things you like or don't like doing.

YOU: Do you like climbing?
FRIEND: Yes, I do.
YOU: So do I.

YOU: Do you like playing football?
FRIEND: No, I don't.
YOU: Neither do I.

53 (fifty-three)

Watersports		Indoor sports		Indoor activities	
Do you like:		Do you like playing:		Do you like:	
windsurfing?	☐	badminton?	☐	working with computers?	☐
water skiing?	☐	table tennis?	☐	acting?	☐
scuba diving?	☐	volleyball?	☐	painting?	☐
canoeing?	☐			doing gymnastics?	☐
sailing?	☐			dancing?	☐
				visiting museums?	☐

4 Talk about the things you can or can't do.

YOU: Can you windsurf?
FRIEND: Yes, I can.
YOU: So can I.

YOU: Can you water ski?
FRIEND: No, I can't.
YOU: Neither can I.

5 Choose two members of your family and write what each of them likes and doesn't like doing.

My brother George likes … but he doesn't like …. My mother …

Joke time!

CUSTOMER: Waiter! Waiter! I don't like this cheese.
WAITER: Why don't you like it, sir?
CUSTOMER: There are holes in it.
WAITER: Well, eat the cheese and leave the holes on your plate.

LESSON 35 Roundup

Read

TARETA · LIVES · ON · AN · ISLAND

Tareta Riki is thirteen years old. She is Polynesian and lives on the little island of Aitutaki in the south of the central Pacific Ocean. Aitutaki is one of a group of islands called the Cook Islands.

Tareta has two sisters and a brother. Her mother is a customs officer at the airport and her father is an ambulance driver at the island hospital. Her elder brother doesn't live at home. He is married and lives in New Zealand.

Tareta goes to school on the island. 'I like most subjects. I like learning new things. My favourite subject is physics but I also like gymnastics and volleyball. We have homework to do every evening.

At home in the evenings I like cooking and making clothes. At the weekend, on Saturday, I have dancing classes. I love dancing and listening to music.'

Which is the best answer?

1. Paragraph 1 is about Tareta's:
   a) island home.
   b) family.
   c) the Pacific Ocean.
2. Paragraph 2 is about:
   a) her friends.
   b) her job.
   c) her family.
3. Paragraph 3 is mainly about:
   a) sport.
   b) her school subjects.
   c) her free time activities.
4. Paragraph 4 is about:
   a) her free time activities.
   b) her homework.
   c) Saturday and Sunday.

Write

Tareta is your penfriend. Write a letter to her. Use the letter in Lesson 24 to help you.

Paragraph 1
Introduce yourself: give your age and nationality, and say where you live.

Paragraph 2
Tell Tareta about your family: say who they are and what their jobs are.

Paragraph 3
Tell Tareta about your school and your favourite school subjects. Say which days of the week they are on.

Paragraph 4
Tell her about your favourite sports and activities. Also say what you like doing in the evenings.

Finish your letter with

Looking forward to hearing from you.
Best wishes,

Conversation

Complete the conversation with Andy.

ANDY: We've got Maths every day except Friday. What about you?
YOU: ....
ANDY: When have you got Games?
YOU: ....
ANDY: What sports do you like?
YOU: ....
ANDY: There's a super new hamburger bar near our school. Do you like hamburgers?
YOU: ....
ANDY: I like chocolate milkshakes. Which flavour do you like?
YOU: ....
ANDY: Anyway, I must go. It's time for my music lesson. Bye. See you!
YOU: ....

Listen

Listen to Melanie talking about her school subjects and on which days she has them. Copy the chart and make notes to complete it.

Name	Age	Favourite subjects	Days

Project

In your class, what are the three most popular:

school subjects?   outdoor sports?
indoor activities?

Grammar Lessons 31-35

Do you like	hamburgers? swimming? these/those shorts?

| Yes, | I | do. |
| No, | | don't. |

Do you want	mustard? onions?

Which	sports bag one trainers ones	do you like?

| I like | this/that the red | one. |
| | these/those. the red ones. | |

I like He/She likes	cheeseburgers. tea. swimming.

So do I.

I don't He/She doesn't	like	mustard. playing tennis.

Neither do I.

I can swim.   So can I.   I can't skate.   Neither can I.

When have we got Maths?

We've got Maths on	Monday.	
	Tuesday	morning. afternoon.

Have we got Maths on Friday?

| Yes, | we | have. |
| No, | | haven't. |

LESSON 36 — A big golden Labrador.

My Pets

We have got three family pets: a dog, a cat and a tortoise. The dog's name is Big Ben. He is a big golden Labrador. He is beautiful. He has got big brown eyes and a long tail. He is a very friendly dog but he is sometimes a bit stupid. Dogs are expensive to keep but they are very good guards for the house.

Our cat is called Cleopatra. She is quite young but she is not a kitten. She is very pretty. She has got black and white fur and green eyes. She's clever, too, and very clean.

The tortoise's name is Rocky. He has got short, fat legs, a long neck and a very hard shell. He is also very old and slow. He's ugly and dirty but I like him.

1 Read Kate's composition. Answer about the pets.

Answer about Big Ben.

1. Is Big Ben small?
   No, he isn't. He's big.

1. Is Big Ben small?
2. What sort of dog is he?
3. Is he ugly?
4. What colour are his eyes?
5. Is his tail short?
6. Is he unfriendly?
7. Is he a clever dog?
8. Are dogs cheap pets?

Answer about Cleopatra.

1. Is she a kitten?
2. Is she ugly?
3. Is she dirty?

Answer about Rocky.

1. What sort of animal is Rocky?
2. Are Rocky's legs long and thin?
3. Is his shell soft?
4. Is he young?

1. GIRAFFE (AFRICA)
2. SPIDER MONKEY (SOUTH AMERICA)
3. KOALA BEAR (AUSTRALIA)
4. ANTEATER (SOUTH AMERICA)
5. GIANT CRAB (ASIA)
6. LEOPARD (AFRICA)
7. ZEBRA (AFRICA)

2 In pairs, find an animal with one of the following:

a long tongue   long arms
a small nose   soft fur
a hard shell   thin legs
a short tail   small spots
a long neck   big spots
small ears   black and white stripes

3 Talk about the animals.

YOU: What's special about a giraffe?
FRIEND: It's got a very long neck, long thin legs and small ears.

4 Write about the animals.

1. This is a giraffe. It has long thin legs, a very long neck and small ears. It lives in Africa.

5 Guess the animal.

One person thinks of an animal. The other person must ask questions to guess which animal it is.

YOU: What's it like?
FRIEND: It's black and white. It's got big spots and small ears and it lives in China.
YOU: I know! It's a panda.

LESSON 37 It's too high!

Dialogue

LUCY: Look! That nasty dog from next door is chasing Cleo!
ANDY: Cleo's in the tree. She can't get down. Be quiet, you noisy dog!
JOHN: It's no good. I can't reach her. It's too dangerous. Help!
ANDY: What's the matter?
JOHN: I'm frightened! I'm slipping!
ANDY: Hang on to the branch and move along it. It's easy! It's quite safe!
JOHN: No, I'm too heavy.
ANDY: Let go and drop.
JOHN: It's too high!
ANDY: Help! Help! Someone bring a ladder!

1 True or False?

1. The dog next door is a nice dog.
2. The dog is chasing the cat.
3. The cat can't get down.
4. The cat is slipping.
5. Andy and John are in the tree.
6. John can reach the cat.
7. The branch is low.

2 Look at the pictures below and ask and say what the matter is.

1. YOU: What's the matter?
   FRIEND: It's too difficult.
2. YOU: What's the matter?
   FRIEND: It's too hot.

Choose from this list:
heavy easy hot small long noisy cold big
short difficult high dangerous low light

3 Write sentences to say what you think of:

1. your school day
   Our school day is too long.

1. your school day
2. your school holidays
3. your exams
4. your village/town/capital city

Joke time!

Tell me about your exam questions.

The questions are very easy. But the answers are too difficult!

LESSON 38 Speak loudly and clearly!

Dialogue

KATE: Dad, I need some help with my French speech.
MR MORGAN: OK. Go on.
KATE: 'Bonjour...' Wait a moment! The TV's too loud.
MR MORGAN: Turn it off. It isn't very interesting.
KATE: 'Bonjour...'
MR MORGAN: No, you're speaking too quietly. I can't hear you. Speak loudly.
KATE: 'Bonjour, Mesdames et Messieurs, je suis...'
MR MORGAN: Stop! Now you're speaking too fast! Speak slowly and clearly.
KATE: 'Bon-jour, Mes-dam-es et Mes-sieurs je-...'
MR MORGAN: That's too slow now.
KATE: OK. What about this? 'Good evening Ladies and Gentlemen. I am very happy to welcome you to our school in Dover.'
MR MORGAN: That's very nice!
KATE: Oh Dad!

1 Complete these sentences with words from the dialogue.

1. The television is too ....
2. The television programme is not very ....
3. At first Kate speaks too ... so her father asks her to speak ....
4. Then she speaks too ... so her father asks her to speak ... and ....
5. Then Kate speaks too ....
6. At last her father says her speech is ....

2 Look at the pictures below. In pairs, ask and answer the questions correctly.

YOU: Are they running slowly?
FRIEND: No, they're running fast.

1. Are they running slowly?
2. Are they smiling nastily?
3. Are they walking fast?
4. Are they singing quietly?
5. Is he talking loudly?
6. Is he walking slowly?

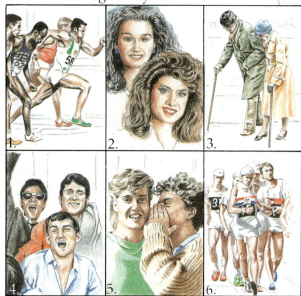

3 Ask different people in the class to do these things.

1. Go to the front of the class slowly.
2. Say *good morning* loudly.
3. Walk towards the door quickly.
4. Shut the door quietly.
5. Go back to your seat slowly.
6. Say your name and address slowly and clearly.
7. Say *thank you* nicely.
8. You are Dracula. Say *Come here my little friend* nastily.

Joke time!

LESSON 39 How tall is it?

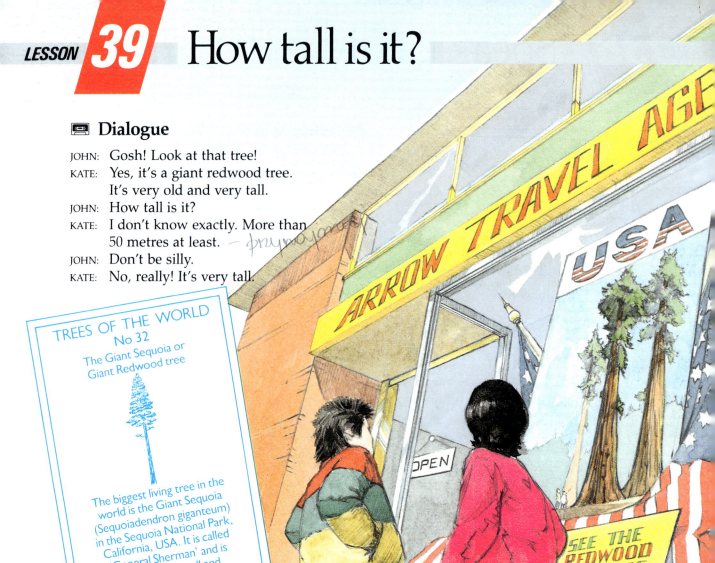

🔊 Dialogue

JOHN: Gosh! Look at that tree!
KATE: Yes, it's a giant redwood tree. It's very old and very tall.
JOHN: How tall is it?
KATE: I don't know exactly. More than 50 metres at least.
JOHN: Don't be silly.
KATE: No, really! It's very tall.

TREES OF THE WORLD
No 32
The Giant Sequoia or Giant Redwood tree

The biggest living tree in the world is the Giant Sequoia (Sequoiadendron giganteum) in the Sequoia National Park, California, USA. It is called 'General Sherman' and is 83.03 metres tall and 24.32 metres wide.

1 Answer the questions.

1. Why are redwood trees special?
2. Where can you see them?
3. How tall is General Sherman?
4. How wide is it?

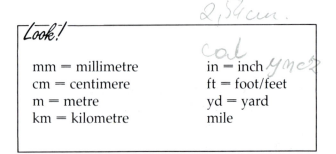

```
mm = millimetre       in = inch
cm = centimere        ft = foot/feet
m = metre             yd = yard
km = kilometre        mile
```

2 Height

YOU: How tall/high is General Sherman?
FRIEND: It's 83.03 metres tall/high.

Ask and answer about the height of famous landmarks.

1. The Eiffel Tower (300.5 m)
2. The Great Pyramid of Giza (146.58 m)
3. The World Trade Center (412.4 m)

Ask and answer about your height.

YOU: How tall are you?
FRIEND: I'm 1 metre 43 centimetres tall.

3 Length

YOU: How long is the Golden Gate Bridge in San Francisco?
FRIEND: It's 1,260 metres long.

Ask and answer about the length of the boats.

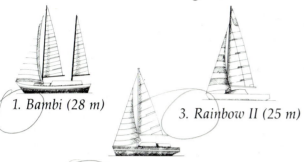

1. Bambi (28 m)
2. Freestyle (30 m)
3. Rainbow II (25 m)

4 Width and depth

YOU: How wide are the Niagara Falls?
FRIEND: They're 750 metres wide.
YOU: How deep is the Pacific Ocean?
FRIEND: It's ... Oh, I don't know!

Ask about the measurements of the swimming pool.

Depth 6m
Length 50m
Width 20m

5 Distance

YOU: How far is it from London to New York?
FRIEND: It's 5,565 kilometres.

You are in Calais. Ask about the distances to different places in Europe.

Paris	314 km
Dover	41 km
London	166 km
Ostend	90 km

6 Quiz

1. How high is Mount Everest?
   Is it a) 8,700 m high?
          b) 4,410 m high?
          c) 5,802 m high?
2. How long is the Amazon River?
   Is it a) 7,100 km long?
          b) 6,300 km long?
          c) 4,400 km long?
3. How far is it from the earth to the moon?
   Is it a) nearly a million kilometres?
          b) nearly half a million kilometres?
          c) nearly a quarter of a million kilometres?
4. How wide is the Grand Canyon?
   Is it a) 29 km wide?
          b) 72 km wide?
          c) 10 km wide?

7 Write about one of the following in your country:

a mountain
a river
a famous building

Give its name and any other interesting facts you know about it. Say how far it is from your home.

8 Measure:

the width of your finger.
the length of your little finger.
the height of your friend.
the distance from your desk to the window.

9 Find out the following information about a swimming pool in your area:

length
width
depth at the deep end and shallow end

LESSON 40 Roundup

Read

REAL LIFE OR *FANTASY*?

Do you like American 'soap operas'? They are called 'real life' stories, but how real are they?

Millions of people all over the world love watching American TV programmes like *Dallas* and *Dynasty*. The names of some of their characters like J.R. and Sue Ellen in *Dallas*, and Alexis and Blake Carrington in *Dynasty* are well known in many countries.

Why are these programmes so popular? Perhaps it's because they are not like real life at all. Nothing is ever ugly or old-fashioned. The women are either young and beautiful or old and beautiful. The men are either clever and good-looking or stupid and good-looking. The people are never fat.

The families are always very rich. They live in very large houses, they drive fast cars and they wear expensive clothes. Nothing in Dallas or Denver is cheap!

DYNASTY

DALLAS

Answer the questions.

How does the article describe:
the women in soap operas?
the men?
the families?
the houses?
the cars?
the clothes?

Write

Write some sentences to explain why American soap operas are not like real life. Write a sentence about each of the topics above. Use *too* with an adjective in each sentence. **Begin:**
The women are too beautiful.

40

Conversation

Complete the conversation with Kate. You are talking on the telephone.

KATE: Hello. It's me again. Tell me, where do you live?
YOU: ....
KATE: Wait a moment! I can't hear. Say it again loudly and clearly.
YOU: ....
KATE: OK. Thanks. Is it a big place?
YOU: ....
KATE: What's your school like?
YOU: ....
KATE: Are you a noisy class?
YOU: ....
KATE: Do you think English is easy?
YOU: ....
KATE: Anyway, I must go. Bye!
YOU: ....

Listen

Sue, John and Andy are rehearsing for the school play. The drama teacher is helping them. Match the teacher's comments with the correct person.

ANDY... | is speaking too fast.
JOHN... | is not speaking clearly.
SUE... | is speaking too quietly and too slowly.

Joke time!

What's big, hairy and flies at 2,000mph?

King Kongcorde.

Grammar Lessons 36-40

| Is he/she tall? | Are they friendly? | What's it like? |

| It's too | high. difficult. |

| It's | very / not very / quite | easy. |

| It's got/It has | a long nose. very short ears. |

| He/She is walking | too / very | quickly. |

| Open / Walk to | the door | slowly. quietly. |

| How far is it from New York to London? | It's 5,565 km. |

| How tall | are you? is Andy? is it? | I'm / He's 1 m 50 cm / It's 200 m | tall. |

| How | high / long / wide / deep | is | General Sherman? the River Amazon? your desk? the swimming pool? | It's | 83.03 m (high). 4,132 miles (long). 320 cm (wide). 7 m (deep). |

Adjectives: quiet nice nasty fast
Adverbs: quietly nicely nastily fast

(sixty-four) 64

LESSON 41 — How much are they?

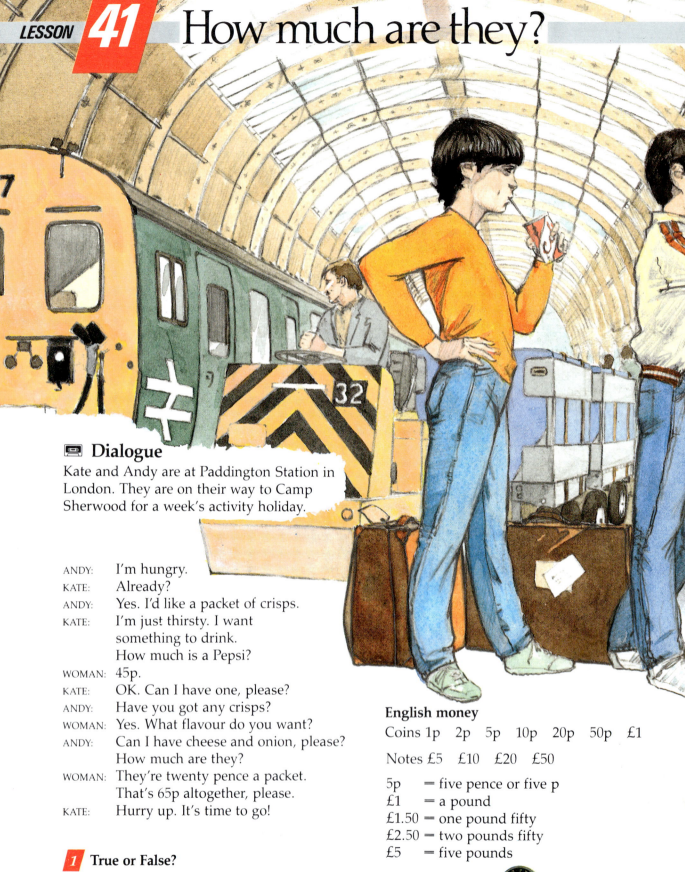

🎧 Dialogue

Kate and Andy are at Paddington Station in London. They are on their way to Camp Sherwood for a week's activity holiday.

ANDY: I'm hungry.
KATE: Already?
ANDY: Yes. I'd like a packet of crisps.
KATE: I'm just thirsty. I want something to drink. How much is a Pepsi?
WOMAN: 45p.
KATE: OK. Can I have one, please?
ANDY: Have you got any crisps?
WOMAN: Yes. What flavour do you want?
ANDY: Can I have cheese and onion, please? How much are they?
WOMAN: They're twenty pence a packet. That's 65p altogether, please.
KATE: Hurry up. It's time to go!

1 True or False?

1. Andy and Kate are both hungry.
2. Andy wants a packet of crisps.
3. The crisps are 45p a packet.
4. Kate gives the woman 20p.
5. Andy buys two drinks.

English money

Coins 1p   2p   5p   10p   20p   50p   £1

Notes £5   £10   £20   £50

5p   = five pence or five p
£1   = a pound
£1.50 = one pound fifty
£2.50 = two pounds fifty
£5   = five pounds

65 (sixty-five)

2 Ask and answer about the prices of the food and drink in the pictures below.

YOU: How much is a packet of biscuits?
FRIEND: It's 30p.
YOU: How much are the oranges?
FRIEND: They're 19p each.

a packet of biscuits (30p)   *a packet of crisps (20p)*   *a packet of nuts (50p)*

oranges (19p each)   *peaches (25p each)*   *apples (14p each)*

Coke (45p)   *lemonade (45p)*   *orange juice (40p)*

3 In pairs or groups buy things from each other.

YOU: Have you got any biscuits?
FRIEND: Yes, I have.
YOU: How much are they?
FRIEND: They're thirty pence a packet.
YOU: Can I have two packets, please?
FRIEND: Here you are. That's 60p altogether.
YOU: Thank you.

4 Ask and say what you would like to eat and drink.

YOU: I'm hungry. I'd like something to eat.
FRIEND: What do you want? I've got biscuits and crisps.
YOU: I'd like some crisps, please.

LESSON 42 What time is it?

🔊 Dialogue

KATE: What time does the train arrive?
DAVE: At six o'clock. Are you tired?
KATE: No, I'm just bored. What time is it now?
DAVE: It's half past five.
KATE: Gosh, it's a long journey.
ANDY: When's supper?
DAVE: You're lucky. It's early tonight. It's at half past six. It's usually at seven o'clock.
ANDY: Hurry up, you stupid train. I'm hungry!

1 Complete the sentences with the correct time.

1. The train arrives at ....
2. The time is now ....
3. Supper at Camp Sherwood tonight is at ....
4. Supper at Camp Sherwood is usually at ....

2 Say these clock times below.

 7.00 seven o'clock
 7.05 five past seven
 7.10 ten past seven

 7.15 quarter past seven
 7.20 twenty past seven
 7.25 twenty-five past seven

 7.30 half past seven
 7.35 twenty-five to eight
 7.40 twenty to eight

 7.45 quarter to eight
 7.50 ten to eight
 7.55 five to eight

3 Ask and answer about the times.

YOU: What time is it?
FRIEND: It's half past nine.

1.   2.   3.

4.   5.

4 Use the timetable below to ask and answer about different train times.

YOU: What time does the train leave?
FRIEND: At eleven minutes past eight.
YOU: What time does the train arrive?
FRIEND: At one minute past nine.

🚆 **British Rail**: Windsor station and Safari park	
Waterloo ..... depart 8.11	Windsor ..... arrive 9.01
8.42	9.30
9.12	10.04
9.42	10.30
10.12	11.00

5 Answer the questions about you.

What time is your supper?
It's at ....
What time is your bedtime?
What time is your first lesson of the day?
What time are your English lessons?

LESSON 43 It's raining.

🎧 Dialogue

KATE: Can we go out and play volleyball?
LOUISE: No! It's raining.
ANDY: No, it isn't. The sun's shining. Look, up there behind the clouds. I can see the sun.
KATE: Yes, I can see it too.
LOUISE: Well, I can't. Anyway, it's Letter Writing Hour on the timetable. OK? Are you all writing a letter to your parents?
CHILDREN: Yes, we are.

The weather

rain *snow* *sun* *cloud*

1. It's raining.
   It's wet.

2. It's cloudy.
   It's dull.

3. It's snowing.
   It's cold.
   It's freezing.

4. The sun is shining.
   It's hot.
   It's warm and sunny.

2 Ask and say what the weather is like in each of the pictures above.

YOU: What's the weather like in picture 1?
FRIEND: It's raining./It's wet.

3 Ask and answer more questions about the weather in the pictures.

YOU: Is it snowing/raining in picture 1?
FRIEND: No, it isn't./Yes, it is.

1 Answer the questions.

1. What do Kate and Andy want to do?
2. What's the weather like?
3. Where's the sun?
4. What are the children doing?

4 About your weather.

1. Ask and say what the weather's like outside at the moment.
2. On average, how many:
   centimetres of rain do you get in December?
   hours of sunshine do you get in August?

LESSON 44 We have supper at seven.

PO Box 12, Taunton, Somerset

CAMP SHERWOOD

Monday

Dear Mum and Dad,
How are you? The camp is o.k. The weather is horrible. It is raining. We are all writing letters. What's the weather like at home?

We get up every morning at a quarter to eight and have a shower. The water is always cold. It's really horrible! Then we get dressed and have breakfast at half past eight. Breakfast is nice. We have three different sorts of cereal, bacon and eggs, toast and marmalade and tea.

After breakfast we go riding or canoeing. We have a morning break at eleven o'clock. We usually have orange juice and biscuits. Then we have free activities.

1 Ask and answer about what time Kate and Andy do things.

YOU: What time do Kate and Andy get up?
FRIEND: They get up at a quarter to eight.

1. get up?
2. have a shower and get dressed?
3. have breakfast?
4. have lunch?
5. have supper?
6. go to bed?

2 Copy Kate and Andy's daily diary at Camp Sherwood. Complete it with information from the letter.

DAILY DIARY

Morning programme	Afternoon programme
7.45 We get up and	14.30
8.30	16.00
9.15	16.30
11.00	19.00
11.30 We have free activities,	19.45 We watch a video or
13.30	21.30

We have lunch at half past one. We have hamburgers and chips or fish and chips but the chips aren't very nice. In the afternoon we usually play football or volleyball. Tea is at four o'clock and after tea we ride on the mini motorbikes. They're great!

We have supper at seven. After supper we watch a video (usually Tom and Jerry!) or have a disco. We can play our own cassettes. Bedtime is at half past nine. I am in a very big room with seven other girls. Our monitor is called Louise but we call her Lulu.

We're both all right and we aren't homesick! (I am a little bit, Andy.)

Love from Kate and Andy.

PS Please send my autograph book.

3 Ask and answer about Kate or Andy's routine at Camp Sherwood.

YOU: What does Kate/Andy do after breakfast?
FRIEND: She/He goes riding or canoeing.

Ask what she/he does after breakfast.
after lunch.
after supper.

Ask what she/he has for breakfast.
for morning break.
for lunch.

4 Make a timetable of your own daily routine and talk about it with your partner.

5 Write some sentences about your day.

6 The coffee-pot game

Think of an activity, like 'have a cold shower' and write it down. Your friends must try to guess what it is, saying the word *coffee-pot* instead of the verb. Remember they can only ask you *Yes/No* questions like:

Are you coffee-potting now?
Can Miss Harris coffee-pot?
Do you coffee-pot in the classroom?
Do you coffee-pot every day?
Do you coffee-pot in the morning?
Do you coffee-pot alone?

Did you know?

Hens in the USA lay about 1,380,000 eggs every minute.

LESSON 45 Roundup

Read

Peter and Jane in Taunton in south-west England

❝ It's spring time now. Today the weather is fine and the sun is shining. In the spring and summer we get up very early. We help our parents on the farm. At about half past seven we have a light breakfast – just orange juice, yoghurt, tea and bread and jam. We sometimes have fruit. On Saturday and Sunday we have bacon, eggs, sausages and tomatoes, with tea and toast. Breakfast is our favourite meal of the day. ❞

Mwende in Mali in West Africa, south of the Sahara desert

❝ Here in Mali it is very hot. It is the rainy season but there is no rain. The crops are dying and everyone is hungry. In the early morning I have some millet porridge or some rice. Sometimes I have some vegetables like beans or onions. I have the same thing every day of the week. ❞

Copy the chart and complete it with information from the texts.

	Peter and Jane	Mwende
Country		
Weather		
Breakfast on a weekday at the weekend		

Listen

Karen works on the TV programme *Breakfast Time*. Listen to her talking about her routine, and complete the timetable.

Time	Activity
......	She gets up and has a cup of coffee.
......	She takes a taxi to the studio.
4.30	....
......	She reads the programme notes.
6.30	The programme starts.
......	She watches a video of the programme.
10.00	She has lunch.

Project

Make a survey of your class. Find out what time people get up and go to bed. Make a graph like the one below for each question.

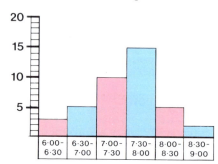

Write

Write a letter to a friend about your daily routine. Use the letter in Lesson 44 to help you.

Paragraph 1
Say what time you get up and what you have for breakfast.

Paragraph 2
Say what you usually do during the day, how many lessons you have and what you do in the breaks.

Paragraph 3
Say what activities you do after school and in the evenings. Say also what time you go to bed.

🅒 Conversation

Complete the conversation with Andy. You are talking on the telephone.

ANDY: Hello. The weather's horrible here today. It's cold and wet. What's the weather like in your area today?
YOU: ....
ANDY: What time do you finish lessons in the afternoon?
YOU: ....
ANDY: What do you usually do after school?
YOU: ....
ANDY: Do you? I usually go to John's house and play table tennis. Anyway, what's the time now?
YOU: ....
ANDY: Is it? I must go. Bye!
YOU: ....

Grammar Lessons 41-45

How much	is	it? / an orange?		It's 45p.		
	are	they? / the oranges?		They're	40p	a packet.
					20p	each.

I'm	hungry. / thirsty.		I'd like something to	eat. / drink.

What do you want?		Can I have / I'd like	some biscuits, / some lemonade,	please.

What time is it?	It's five o'clock.

What time is lunch?	It's at half past twelve.

What time / When	do	you / they	get up? / go to bed?		I / We / They	get up / go to bed	at	eight o'clock. / 9.30.
	does he/she				He/She gets up			

What	do	you / they	do in the	morning? / afternoon? / evening?		I / We / They	usually sometimes	go swimming. / go riding. / play tennis.
	does he/she					He/She		plays tennis. / goes swimming.

What's the weather like?		It's	raining. / very cold.

LESSON 46 What's 'goodbye' in Japanese?

Dialogue

KATE: Look at 16 Across. 'What's *goodbye* in Japanese?'
SUE: What's the first letter?
KATE: It's an S.
SUE: And the last?
KATE: An A.
SUE: Then it's *sayonara*.
KATE: How do you spell it?
SUE: S-A-Y-O-N-A-R-A.
KATE: And how do you pronounce it again?
SUE: Sigh-an-ar-ah.
KATE: It sounds a bit sad.
SUE: Yes, it does. Perhaps it's because it means *goodbye*.

1 Ask and answer about words and phrases from other languages.

YOU: What's *goodbye* in Japanese?
FRIEND: It's *sayonara*./I don't know.

Ask about:

1. *goodbye* in Japanese.
2. *good morning* in French.
3. *good evening* in Greek.
4. *how are you?* in German.
5. *yes* and *no* in Russian.
6. *goodbye* in Spanish.
7. *hotel* in French.

2 Ask and say what words mean in your language.

YOU: What does *nice* mean?
FRIEND: It means . . . .

Ask about:

nice	stupid	happy
angry	pretty	sad
nasty	beautiful	horrible

3 Ask and say how to pronounce words.

YOU: How do you pronounce R-E-S-T-A-U-R-A-N-T?
FRIEND: *Restaurant.*

Ask about:

restaurant	telephone
theatre	chocolate
programme	aeroplane
television	cinema

4 Tongue twisters

Say these sentences very quickly lots of times:

Lovely little Lucy is licking a large lollipop.

She sells shoes, sandwiches and fish and chips in her shop in Sheffield.

5 Are there any English words in your language? How many can you write down in a minute?

LESSON 47 When's your birthday?

🔊 Dialogue

KATE: When's your birthday?
SUE: It's in March. When's yours?
KATE: Mine's in the summer. It's on 22nd July.
SUE: What's the date today?
KATE: It's 11th May.
SUE: Oh, it's Miss Harris's birthday next Thursday. Let's collect some money and get her a present.
KATE: And a card!
SUE: OK. Let's tell the others ...
MRS TODD: Susan! Kate! This is a PE class, not a conversation class!

1 Answer the questions.

1. In which month is Sue's birthday?
2. In which season is Kate's birthday?
3. In which month is Kate's birthday?
4. On which day of the week is Miss Harris's birthday?

2 Use the calendar. Ask and say in which months people's birthdays are.

YOU: When's Kate's birthday?
FRIEND: It's in July. When's John's?
YOU: In September.

3 Practise saying the ordinal numbers.

1st first	2nd second	3rd third	4th fourth	5th fifth	6th sixth
7th seventh	8th eighth	9th ninth	10th tenth	11th eleventh	12th twelfth
13th thirteenth	14th fourteenth	15th fifteenth	16th sixteenth	17th seventeenth	18th eighteenth
19th nineteenth	20th twentieth	21st twenty-first	29th twenty-ninth	30th thirtieth	31st thirty-first

Look!

in March   **on** 14th March
We write *14th March*,
but we say '**the** fourteenth **of** March'.

4 Look at the calendar again and ask and answer about the dates of people's birthdays.

YOU: When's Ben's birthday?
FRIEND: It's on 6th January.

5 In groups, ask the dates of people's birthdays and make a birthday calendar for the class.

YOU: When's your birthday?
FRIEND: It's on 4th September.

The seasons in Britain

Spring	Summer	Autumn	Winter
March	June	September	December
April	July	October	January
May	August	November	February

LESSON 48 My sister never helps!

always · usually · often
sometimes · never
I **always** make my bed.

🎧 Dialogue

KATE: What's the matter? Why are you sad?
JOHN: I'm not sad! I'm angry! I haven't got my pocket money this week.
KATE: Why not?
JOHN: My mum says I'm lazy and I don't help in the house.
KATE: Do you want some crisps?
JOHN: Thanks. It's not true. I help my mum quite a lot. My sister never helps! But I do.
KATE: I don't believe you!
JOHN: Well, I usually make my bed.

1 Correct the statements.

1. John is happy.
   No. He's angry.

1. John is happy.
2. John has got his pocket money this week.
3. John's sister helps in the house.
4. John always makes his bed.

2 Copy and complete the questionnaire on the right for yourself and for your partner.

YOU: Do you ever make your bed?
FRIEND: Yes, always.

3 Tell the class about one or two things you do in the house and how you spend your pocket money.

JOHN: I usually make my bed and I sometimes tidy my room. I never buy clothes with my pocket money.

4 Say how much John helps in the house.

YOU: He usually makes his bed.
FRIEND: And he sometimes tidies his room.

Now say what he does with his pocket money.

YOU: He never buys clothes.
FRIEND: And he never buys records or cassettes.

Do you help in the house? (Tell the truth!)

PART 1: JOBS

Do you ever
1. make your bed?
2. tidy your room?
3. lay the table?
4. do the washing up?
5. take the rubbish out?

PART 2: POCKET MONEY

6. Do you get pocket money?

What do you do with your pocket money?

Do you ever
7. buy clothes or make-up?
8. buy records or cassettes?
9. buy sweets and icecream?
10. play video games?
11. buy comics or magazines?
12. save it or spend it all?

JOHN	YOU	YOUR FRIEND
1. usually		
2. sometimes		
3. never		
4. sometimes		
5. often (at the weekend)		
6. Yes, once a week		
7. never		
8. never		
9. always		
10. never		
11. often		
12. sometimes		

5 Look at what John says.

'I help my mother quite a lot in the house. I usually make my bed and I sometimes tidy my room – usually on Saturday morning. I sometimes do the washing up and often take the rubbish out at the weekend.

I usually get pocket money once a week. I always buy a few sweets and icecream. I never spend it on clothes or records or cassettes but I often buy comics. I sometimes save a little because I want to buy a canoe.'

Now write two paragraphs about John.

John helps his mother quite a lot in the house.

6 Write one paragraph about the jobs you do and don't do in the house, and another paragraph about how you spend your pocket money.

LESSON 49 — Does she like chocolates?

🔊 Dialogue

SUE: What shall we buy Miss Harris for her birthday? Does she like chocolates?
KATE: Yes, she does. But that's not a very interesting present.
SUE: She likes house plants. Let's get her a rubber plant.
KATE: How much are they?
SUE: Look, they're £6. They're too expensive.
KATE: Let's get her some writing paper and envelopes. She likes writing letters.
SUE: OK. That's £2.20. We've got an extra 50p.
KATE: Hey, Sue! Let's get her a vampire bat as well!

1 True or False?

Miss Harris:
1. doesn't like chocolates.
2. likes house plants.
3. doesn't like writing letters.

2 Find out what your partner likes and doesn't like.

YOU: Do you like yogurt?
FRIEND: Yes, I do./No, I don't.

FOOD AND DRINK

yogurt   milk chocolate   fish soup

INTERESTS

computer games   ballet   classical music

ANIMALS AND REPTILES

snakes   rats   crocodiles

3 Ask someone else in the class about their partner.

YOU: Does Peter like milk chocolate?
FRIEND: No, he doesn't.

4 Look at what Sue writes about Miss Harris.

Miss Harris likes chocolates, houseplants and opera. She doesn't like pop music or dogs.

Write similar sentences about your friend's likes and dislikes.

5 Choose a birthday present for Kate, Andy, Mr Green and Miss Harris.

YOU: It's Kate's/Andy's birthday next week. What shall we get her/him?
FRIEND: Let's get her/him a present.
YOU: What sort of present?
FRIEND: Let's get her/him a jigsaw.
YOU: No, let's get her/him a game.

a scarf   a jigsaw   a mug   a game

a box of   a house   a brush and   tights
chocolates plant   comb set

6 The hidden present

Sue and Kate buy another small present for Miss Harris. Write down the first letter of each item to find out what the present is.

1.   2.   3.   4.

5.   6.   7.   8.

Birthday song

Happy birthday to you!
Happy birthday to you!
Happy birthday Miss Harris!
Happy birthday to you!

LESSON 50 Roundup

Read

Discoveries meets... ANNE McCRODDEN
TRAINEE ENGINEER

When Anne gets up in the morning she puts on an overall and big boots and she carries a helmet—because she's training to be an engineer.

'I am a trainee on a three-year course. I am now in my third year. I am enjoying the course very much. I like making things and I like technical subjects. I think I'm lucky to have something to do. A lot of people think it's strange for a girl to be an engineer. I don't. A lot of my friends laugh at me, but they either have very boring jobs or they are unemployed.

After work at nights I like going to discos and night clubs. I always tell the boys I'm an engineer. They are sometimes rude and say, "Where are your overalls, Jack?" and walk away, but I don't mind. I usually go to the disco with the boys from my course. *They* laugh because I am wearing evening clothes.

At the end of my course I want a job with London Transport because I like trains. Do you know what I want for my birthday? A new helmet!'

Choose the correct answer.

1. When Anne gets dressed she:
   a) puts on a dress.
   b) puts on an overall.

2. Anne:
   a) likes her course very much.
   b) thinks her course is strange.

3. People laugh at Anne because:
   a) she is funny.
   b) they think engineering is a strange job for a girl.

4. Some of Anne's other friends:
   a) have no job.
   b) are boring.

5. In discos, boys are:
   a) usually rude to Jack.
   c) sometimes rude to Anne.

Write

1. Write about the daily routine of an adult you know – a parent, a relative or a friend of the family. Or imagine the life of a famous person.

Paragraph 1
Say what time the person gets up and what he or she usually has for breakfast.
Paragraph 2
Write three or four sentences about what the person does during the day.
Paragraph 3
Say one or two things about the person's routine in the evening and say what he or she has for supper.
or
2. Describe how you usually spend your birthday.

🔊 Conversation

Complete the conversation with John.

JOHN: When's your birthday?
YOU: ....
JOHN: Mine's next month. I want a tent for my birthday. What do you want for yours?
YOU: ....
JOHN: Do you? How much pocket money do you get a week?
YOU: ....
JOHN: What do you do with it?
YOU: ....
JOHN: I buy comics and sweets! I get more money if I help my mother in the house. Do you help in the home?
YOU: ....
JOHN: Does your mother tidy your room?
YOU: ....
JOHN: Oh, there's my dad calling me. Bye!
YOU: ....

🔊 Listen

Listen to Jenny and Mickey talking about jobs in the house. Look at the list below and tick the jobs which they do.

take the rubbish out
go shopping
make the beds
take the dog for a walk
tidy her/his room
wash up
lay the table
do some cooking

Grammar Lessons 46-50

What date is / When's	your birthday?

It's	in	October. / the summer.
	on	Monday. / October 10th.

What's	the	date	today?

It's	Monday, July 3rd. / July 3rd. / 3rd July.

Do you	ever / always / often	help in the home?

I / She / He	always / usually / often / sometimes / never	make my / makes her / makes his	bed.

Does he/she like cats?	Yes, / No,	he/she	does. / doesn't.

He/She	likes / doesn't like	cats.

What shall we	buy / get	Miss Harris/her? / Mr Green/him?

Let's	buy / get	Miss Harris/her / Mr Green/him	a present.

What's / What does	*au revoir*	in English? / mean in English?

It's / It means	goodbye.

(eighty) 80

Oral exercises

LESSONS 1-5

1. Greet and say goodbye to people
Say hello to Kate.
Hello, Kate.
Say goodbye to John.
Goodbye, John.

1. Kate
2. John
3. Cleo
4. Miss Harris
5. Mr Green
6. Mrs Morgan

2. Greet someone and introduce yourself (Open exercise)
Greet Kate.
Hello, Kate. (I'm Mary.)

1. Kate
2. Mr Green
3. Mrs Morgan
4. Miss Harris
5. John
6. Andy

3. Introduce yourself and ask someone's name
You are John.
I'm John. What's your name?

1. John
2. Max
3. Tina
4. Mary
5. Peter

4. Introduce your family to Tina
Introduce your mother.
Hi, Tina. This is my mother.

1. mother
2. father
3. little brother
4. sister

5. Introduce yourself
Hello.
Hello. I'm Tina's brother.

1. Tina/brother
2. John/mother
3. Pat/teacher
4. Anna/teacher
5. Pat/father
6. Anna/friend

6. Give people's names
Who's that?
That's Prince Charles.
What's his name?
That's Stevie Wonder.

1. Prince Charles
2. Stevie Wonder
3. Margaret Thatcher
4. Princess Diana
5. Michael Jackson
6. Tarzan

LESSONS 6-10

1. Ask for personal information
What's your telephone number?
It's 149623.
What's Mary's favourite number?
It's 7.

1. Your telephone number?
2. Mary's favourite number?
3. Andy's address?
4. Kate's favourite number?
5. Jack's address?
6. Tina's telephone number?

2. Ask people's age
Is she six?
No, but she's nearly six.

1. she six?
2. he eleven?
3. you twelve?
4. your brother sixteen?
5. your sister nine?
6. your father forty?

3. Ask how old people are
How old is Tina?
She's twelve.

1. Tina?
2. he?
3. she?
4. Miss Harris?
5. Mark?

4. Answer questions about objects
Is number one a computer?
Yes, it is.
Is number two a pen?
No, it isn't. It's a pencil.

1. computer/yes
2. pen/no/pencil
3. comic/no/notebook
4. cat/yes
5. ruler/no/rubber
6. calculator/yes

5. Identify objects
What's that?
It's my ruler.

1. my ruler
2. Andy's pen
3. Kate's notebook
4. my calculator
5. Sue's cassette recorder
6. Mr Green's pen

6. Give information about animals
What's that animal?
It's an African elephant.

1. African elephant
2. Chinese panda
3. American bald eagle
4. Indian tiger
5. English sheep dog

LESSONS 11-15

1. Say where people are from
Where's Eddie Murphy from?
He's from the USA.

1. Eddie Murphy/USA
2. Isabelle Huppert/France
3. Sophia Loren/Italy
4. Severiano Ballesteros/Spain
5. Daley Thompson/Britain

2. Correct information about nationalities
Is Harrison Ford British?
No, he isn't. He's American.

1. Harrison Ford/American
2. Sophia Loren/Italian
3. Daley Thompson/British
4. Isabelle Huppert/French
5. Severiano Ballesteros/Spanish

3. Say where places are
Where's Peking?
It's in China.

1. Peking/China
2. Rio de Janeiro/Brazil
3. Buenos Aires/Argentina
4. Tokyo/Japan
5. Munich/West Germany

4. Ask about nationalities
Are you Spanish?
No, we aren't. We're Greek.

1. Spanish?
2. American?
3. Italian?
4. Brazilian?
5. Argentinian?

5. Make suitable responses (Open exercise)
Sorry.
(That's OK.)

1. Sorry.
2. Here you are.
3. Goodbye.
4. Thanks very much.
5. Do you want a chocolate?

6. Offer people things
Offer your friend a chocolate.
Do you want a chocolate?

1. a chocolate?
2. some crisps?
3. some sweets?
4. an icecream?
5. some chewing gum?

7. Say what the colours are
What colour is Pat's hair?
It's blonde.
What colour are her eyes?
They're blue.

1. Pat's hair/blonde
2. her eyes/blue
3. Peter's hair/black
4. his eyes/brown
5. Anna's hair/blonde
6. her eyes/green

Oral exercises

LESSONS 16-20

1. Ask whose belongings you have
sweater
Whose sweater is this?
trainers
Whose trainers are these?

1. sweater?
2. trainers?
3. jacket?
4. socks?
5. shoes?
6. anorak?

2. Correct information about belongings
Is this Jane's?
No, it isn't hers. It's mine.
Are these John's?
No, they aren't his. They're mine.

1. this Jane's
2. these John's
3. this Linda's
4. these Robert's
5. this Kate's
6. this Andy's

3. Agree with people's tastes
I like Harrison Ford.
Yes, I like him, too.
I like Nastassia Kinski.
Yes, I like her, too.

1. Harrison Ford
2. Nastassia Kinski
3. The Jackson Five
4. Wham!
5. Sophia Loren
6. Stevie Wonder

4. Say who you like and don't like
I like Michael Jackson. I think he's terrific.
Oh, I don't like him. I think he's horrible.
I don't like Madonna. I think she's boring.
Oh, I like her. I think she's fantastic.

1. I like Michael Jackson. I think he's terrific.
2. I don't like Madonna. I think she's boring.
3. I like Julian Lennon. I think he's terrific.
4. I don't like Billy Idol. I think he's boring.
5. I like Tina Turner. I think she's terrific.
6. I don't like Adam Ant. I think he's boring.

5. Say what you've got and what you haven't got
stamps and badges
I've got some stamps but I haven't got any badges.

1. stamps/badges
2. records/posters
3. French stamps/Italian stamps
4. foreign postcards/foreign coins
5. sweets/crisps

6. Make an offer or a refusal
Have you got any postcards?
Yes, I have. Do you want one?
Have you got any stamps?
No, I haven't. Sorry.

1. postcards/yes
2. stamps/no
3. pencils/yes
4. crisps/yes
5. chocolates/no
6. sweets/no

7. Ask how many
She's got lots of stamps.
Oh? How many has she got?
I've got lots of records.
Oh? How many have you got?

1. She/stamps
2. I/records
3. Jack/videos
4. Anna/posters
5. Mary/badges
6. I/pets

LESSONS 21-25

Ask about numbers
How many people are there in your family?
There are six.

1. people/in your family?
2. students/in your class?
3. girls/in your class?
4. boys/in your class?
5. teachers/in your school?
6. posters/in your bedroom?

2. Ask about rooms in a house
Is there a kitchen in your house?
Yes, there is.

1. kitchen?
2. dining room?
3. attic?
4. bathroom?
5. play room?
6. sitting room?

3. Talk about the furniture in a room
Is there a bed?
Oh yes, there's a very nice bed.
Are there any curtains?
Oh yes, there are some very nice curtains.

1. bed
2. curtains
3. table
4. posters
5. chairs
6. cupboard

4. Comment on places
Are there any castles in France?
Yes, there are some beautiful castles in France.

1. castles in France
2. churches in London
3. gardens in Paris
4. cliffs in Dover
5. Roman remains in Italy
6. places to see in your country

5. Talk about places
Tell me about Canterbury.
It's a city in the south-east of England.
Tell me about Los Angeles.
It's a city on the west coast of the USA.

1. Canterbury/south-east/England
2. Los Angeles/west coast/USA
3. Aberdeen/east coast/Scotland
4. Cambridge/east/England
5. Bordeaux/south-west coast/France
6. Cardiff/south coast/Wales

6. Answer personal questions
(Open exercise)
What's your name, please?
(John Smith.)

1. What's your name, please?
2. What's your address?
3. And your telephone number?
4. Where are you from?
5. How old are you?
6. What are your parents' names?
7. What colour is your hair?
8. What colour are your eyes?

LESSONS 26-30

1. Spell words in English
(Open exercise)
Spell the name of your country.
(E-N-G-L-A-N-D)

1. the name of your country
2. the name of your capital city
3. your best friend's surname
4. your first name
5. the name of your favourite pop singer or group

2. Ask what people are doing
I'm listening to records.
Are you? What are you listening to?
I'm reading.
Are you? What are you reading?

1. listening to records
2. reading
3. watching TV
4. writing
5. eating
6. drinking

82

Oral exercises

3. Give short answers
Are they doing their homework?
Yes, they are.
Is she playing basketball?
No, she isn't.

1. they/do homework/yes
2. she/play basketball/no
3. he/play with dog/yes
4. they/watch TV/no
5. she/make model trains/no
6. he/ride bike/yes

4. Say what people are doing
What are they doing?
They're singing.
What's he doing?
He's running.

1. They   4. He
2. He   5. They
3. She   6. They

LESSONS 31-35

1. Ask what people like
Ask Andy about cheeseburgers.
Do you like cheeseburgers, Andy?

1. cheeseburgers, Andy?
2. mustard, Kate?
3. chocolate milkshakes, Lucy?
4. milk, Sue?
5. tomato ketchup, John?
6. fish, Tom?

2. Say what you like (Open exercise)
Do you like hamburgers with onions?
(Yes, I do.)
Do you like coffee?
(No, I don't.)

1. hamburgers   4. tea without sugar?
   with onions?   5. tomato ketchup?
2. coffee?   6. lots of pepper on
3. bananas?   your food?

3. Ask people to identify the objects they like
Oh, look, that tracksuit's nice.
Which one do you mean?
Oh, look, those trainers are good.
Which ones do you mean?

1. tracksuit/nice   4. anorak/nice
2. trainers/good   5. shoes/good
3. T-shirt/nice   6. school bag/nice

4. Say what people like and don't like
Tina
Tina likes chips but she doesn't like fish.

1. Tina/chips/fish
2. Jack/hamburgers/cheeseburgers
3. Max/milk/tea
4. Mrs Brown/sailing/swimming
5. Mr Brown/skiing/waterskiing
6. Anna/Tina/Jack

5. Ask about your school timetable
English
When have we got English?
Science on Friday
Have we got Science on Friday?

1. When/English?   4. Have/Games
2. Have/Science   on Thursday?
   on Friday?   5. When/Music?
3. Have/Biology   6. When/Maths?
   on Monday?

6. Answer about your school timetable
   (Open exercise)
Have you got English on Thursday?
(Yes, we have.)
Have you got Maths every day?
(No, we haven't.)

1. Have you got English on Thursday?
2. Have you got Maths every day?
3. Have you got Music on Tuesday?
4. Have you got Science on Friday?
5. Have you got History on Wednesday?
6. Have you got English today?

7. Answer about your interests
   (Open exercise)
Do you like canoeing?
(No, I don't.)
Do you like watching TV?
(Yes, I do.)

1. canoeing   4. singing
2. watching TV   5. learning English
3. writing letters   6. doing Maths

8. Talk about your interests and activities (Open exercise)
What subjects to you like learning at school?
(I like learning Geography and English.)

1. What subjects do you like learning at school?
2. What do you like doing at the weekend?
3. What do you like doing after school?
4. Do you like doing homework?
5. What programmes do you like watching on TV?
6. When you are with your friends, what do you like doing?

LESSONS 36-40

1. Give a different opinion
I think it's a beautiful picture.
Oh, I don't think it's beautiful. I think it's ugly.

1. picture/beautiful/ugly
2. man/clever/stupid
3. woman/nice/horrid
4. toy/expensive/cheap
5. car/fast/slow
6. house/small/big

2. Say what the matter is with things
What's the matter with your tea?
It's too hot.

1. tea/too hot   4. chair/too hard
2. soup/too cold   5. hotel room/too
3. homework/too   noisy
   difficult

3. Describe how you are doing things
Come on! Do it quickly.
I am doing it quickly!

1. Come on! Do it quickly.
2. Ssh! Sing softly.
3. Come on! Speak loudly.
4. Wait a moment! Say it clearly.
5. Please drive slowly!
6. Ssh! Play quietly!

4. Follow instructions
Say 'Hello' loudly.
HELLO!

1. Say 'Hello' loudly.
2. Say 'Thank you very much' quietly.
3. Say 'No, I don't' slowly.
4. Say 'I hate you' nastily.
5. Say 'Be quiet and go away, Lucy' very quickly.
6. Say the name of your best friend quietly.

Oral exercises

5. Ask questions about size
nice garden
It's a nice garden. How wide is it?
big swimming pool
It's a big swimming pool. How deep is it?

1. nice garden/wide?
2. big swimming pool/deep?
3. big building/tall?
4. big bridge/long?
5. enormous mountain/high?
6. wide river/deep?

LESSONS 41-45

1. Ask for things to eat and drink
Ask for two Cokes.
Can I have two Cokes, please?

1. two Cokes
2. a glass of milk
3. a packet of crisps
4. two bottles of lemonade
5. a chocolate egg
6. a glass of orange juice

2. Say the price of things
How much is the torch?
It's two pounds eighty.
How much are the postcards?
They're twenty p.

1. the torch/£2.80
2. the postcards/20p
3. the writing paper/£1.75
4. a packet of sweets/54p
5. the stickers/10p

3. Give times of arrival
What time does the train arrive?
It arrives at five o'clock.

1. train/five o'clock
2. plane/half past four
3. boat/quarter past four
4. hovercraft/half past three
5. bus/nine o'clock
6. train/quarter past seven

4. Say what time it is
What's the time, please?
It's five to ten.

1.
2.
3.
4.
5.
6.

5. Ask about routines
Glenda is a famous film star. Ask her about her daily timetable.
Ask her what time she gets up.
What time do you get up Miss Glenning?
Get up? How horrible. I get up at half past eleven.

1. What time/get up?
2. What time/have breakfast?
3. Where/have lunch?
4. What/have for lunch?
5. What time/go to the studios?
6. When/go to bed?

6. Answer questions about your daily routine (Open exercise)
What time do you usually get up in the morning?
I usually get up at half past seven.

1. What time do you usually get up in the morning?
2. What about on Saturday and Sunday?
3. Do you get dressed before breakfast or after breakfast?
4. What do you usually have for breakfast?
5. Where do you have lunch?
6. What do you usually do in the evenings?
7. What time do you go to bed?
8. Do you read in bed?

7. Say what the weather is like
What's the weather like in Rome today?
It's sunny.

1. Rome/sunny
2. London/sunny
3. Berlin/cloudy
4. Stockholm/snowing
5. New York/raining
6. Malta/raining

LESSONS 46-50

1. Answer about birthdays
When's Ben's birthday?
It's some time in the winter.
Do you know when?
I think it's in January.

1. Ben/winter/January
2. Carol/spring/May
3. Kate/summer/July
4. John/autumn/September
5. Sue/spring/March
6. Tom/summer/June

2. Give exact dates of birthdays
When's John's birthday?
It's on the third of September.

1. John/3rd September
2. Jamie/21st November
3. Mary/12th January
4. Kevin/31st March
5. Sheila/24th October
6. Mr Morgan/11th December

3. Say what the date is (Open exercise)
What's the date today?
(It's the fifth of April.)

1. What's the date today?
2. What's the date tomorrow?
3. What date's your birthday?
4. What date's your best friend's birthday?
5. What date's your next English class?
6. What date's the start of the school holidays?

4. Ask about the spelling and meaning of words.
How do you spell 'beautiful'?
B-E-A-U-T-I-F-U-L
What does 'intelligent' mean?
That you are clever.

1. How/spell 'beautiful'?
2. What/'intelligent' mean?
3. What/'helmet' mean?
4. How/spell 'technical'?
5. What/'strange' mean?
6. How/spell 'frightened'?

5. Ask about the things Miss Harris likes
Does Miss Harris like plants?
Yes, she does.
Does she like video games?
No, she doesn't.

1. plants?
2. video games?
3. snakes?
4. peanut butter?
5. classical music?
6. chocolate?

Słówka i wyrażenia

Ewa Nanowska *Gdańsk*

Pierwsze tłumaczenie słów angielskich odzwierciedla ich znaczenie w lekcji, w której pojawiają się po raz pierwszy. W nawiasie podane są znaczenia, w których słowa te występują w dalszych lekcjach podręcznika, uwagi dodatkowe, inne znaczenia podstawowe itp.

LEKCJA 1

my mój (moja, moje, mój)
your twój (twoja, twoje, twoi, wasz, wasza, wasze, wasi)
and i (a)
Hello Cześć
name imię (nazwisko lub pełne imię i nazwisko)
What? Co? Jaki? (Jaka?, Jakie?, Jacy?)
be (is) być (jest)
cardinal numbers **1–10** *liczebniki główne 1–10*

LEKCJA 2

Good afternoon Dzień dobry (po południu)
Good evening Dobry wieczór
Good morning Dzień dobry (rano)
Goodbye Do widzenia
friend kolega (przyjaciel)
picture obrazek
teacher nauczyciel
under pod
I ja
be (am) być (jestem)
titles tytuły używane przed nazwiskiem
Miss panna (panno...!)
Mr pan (panie...!)
Mrs pani (pani...!)
family members członkowie rodziny
brother brat
father ojciec
mother matka
sister siostra

LEKCJA 3

OK dobrze (w porządku, zgoda)
little mała (mały, małe, mali, mało)
a (jeden, jakiś, pewien, któryś)
Hi! Czołem (Cześć!)
I'm OK, thanks. Dobrze, dziękuję
no nie
yes tak
dad tata (tato!)
school szkoła
twins bliźniaki
witch wiedźma, czarownica
from z, ze, od
he on
she ona
this to (ten, ta)
we my
you ty (wy)
How? Jak?
go away Odejdź! (Idź sobie!)

know (a person) znać (kogoś)
be (are) być (jesteś)

LEKCJA 4

called nazywany (zwany)
her jej (ja, nią, niej)
his jego
our nasz (nasza, nasi, nasze)
but ale (lecz)
I must go. Muszę iść.
Bye! Cześć (Do zobaczenia, narazie)
cat kot
dog pies
mum mama (Mamo!)
teatime czas na herbatę
that to (tamten, tamta, tamto)
Who? Kto?

LEKCJA 5

me ja (mnie, mi, mną)
have mieć, (mam, masz, mamy, macie, mają)

LEKCJA 6

young młoda (młody, młode, młodzi)
nearly prawie
only dopiero (tylko)
too zbyt, za (też, również)
Come on. No chodź! (No dalej!)
Let's... ...-my! (jak np. w zdaniu: *Let's go!* – Chodźmy!)
years old lat (część zdania np. *I am five years old* – Mam 5 lat.)
How old? Ile lat? (początek pytania: *How old are you?* – Ile masz lat? Również: Ile on/ona/ono/my/wy/oni mają lat?)
go pójść, iść (chodzić)
want chcieć
cardinal numbers **11–20** *liczebniki główne 11–20*

LEKCJA 7

favourite ulubiony
new nowy
old stary
the (ten, ta, to, ci)
Say it again slowly. Powiedz to jeszcze raz wolno.
address book notatnik z adresami
number numer
telephone telefon
it to (on, ona, ono)
look at spójrz na... (patrzeć)
cardinal numbers **20–101** *liczebniki główne 20–101*

LEKCJA 8

book książka
calculator kalkulator
cassette recorder magnetofon kasetowy
chair krzesło
comic komiks
computer komputer
desk biurko
notebook notatnik
pen pióro
pencil ołówek
rubber gumka
ruler linijka
stool taboret, stołek
table stół

LEKCJA 9

big duży
good dobrze! (dobry)
its jego (jej)
You're wrong. Mylisz się (niesłuszny, zły)
Thank you. Dziękuję!
animal zwierzę
ears uszy
knees kolana
page strona
picture obrazek
next następny
Where? Gdzie?
know wiedzieć (wiem)
animals zwierzęta
eagle orzeł
elephant słoń
lion lew
panda panda
sheep dog owczarek (pies pasterski)
tiger tygrys
countries and nationalities kraje i narodowości
Africa (African) Afryka (afrykański)
China (Chinese) Chiny (chiński)
England (English) Anglia (angielski)
India (Indian) Indie (indyjski)
North America (American) Ameryka Północna (amerykański)

LEKCJA 10

wild dziki
today dzisiaj
city miasto
pet zwierzątko domowe
has ma

LEKCJA 11

man (pl men) człowiek/ mężczyzna (ludzie/ mężczyźni)
nationality narodowość
woman (pl women) kobieta, (kobiety)
in w
countries and nationalities kraje i narodowości
Britain (British) Wielka Brytania (brytyjski)
France (French) Francja (francuski)
Italy (Italian) Włochy (włoski)
Spain (Spanish) Hiszpania (hiszpański)
The USA (American) Stany Zjednoczone (amerykański)

LEKCJA 12

silly niemądry (głupi)
It doesn't matter. Nic nie szkodzi. (to nie ma znaczenia)
Look out! Uważaj!
Sorry. Przepraszam!
That's OK. W porządku (już dobrze)
boy chłopiec
children (*sing* child) dzieci (dziecko)
girl dziewczynka
parent rodzic
countries and nationalities kraje i narodowości
Argentina (Argentinian) Argentyna (argentyński)
Brazil (Brazilian) Brazylia (brazylijski)
Germany (German) Niemcy (niemiecki)
Greece (Greek) Grecja (grecki)
Japan (Japanese) Japonia (japoński)
Turkey (Turkish) Turcja (turecki)

LEKCJA 13

some kilka (trochę)
Here you are. Proszę bardzo.
Thanks (very much).
No, thank you. Nie, dziękuję.
Yes, please. Tak, proszę.
for za (dla, przez)
hate nienawidzę (nie znoszę, nie cierpię)
love uwielbiam, kocham
food jedzenie
chewing gum guma do żucia
chocolates czekoladki
crisps prażynki
icecream lody
liquorice cukierki lukrecjowe
sweet cukierek

LEKCJA 14

bright jaskrawy (świetlisty, bystry)
dark ciemny
light jasny (światło, lekki)
apple jabłko
banana banan
cloud chmura
colour kolor
eyes oczy
grass trawa
hair włosy
orange pomarańcz
sea morze

sky niebo
sun słońce
tomato pomidor
tree drzewo
What colour? Jakiego koloru?
colours kolory
black czarny (czarna, czarne)
blonde blond
blue niebieski (niebieska, niebieskie)
brown brązowy (brązowa, brązowe)
grey szary (szara, szare)
orange pomarańczowy
pink różowy
purple liliowy
red czerwony
white biały
yellow żółty

LEKCJA 15
good–looking przystojny (przystojni)
doctor lekarz
schoolgirl uczennica

LEKCJA 16
here tutaj
perhaps być może
Don't be cheeky! Nie bądź taki mądry!
hers jej
his jego
mine mój, moja, moje (moi)
these te, ci
this ten (ta, to)
yours twój (twoja, twoje, twoi)
Whose? Czyj, czyja, czyje?
Why? Dlaczego?
clothes ubrania
anorak anorak (ciepła kurtka)
blouse bluzka
boots kozaki
coat płaszcz
dress sukienka
jacket kurtka, marynarka
jeans dżinsy
shirt koszula
shoes buty
skirt spódnica
socks skarpetki
sweater sweter
trainers adidasy
trousers spodnie
T–shirt bluzka z krótkim rękawkiem

LEKCJA 17
bad zły (zła, złe, źli)
boring nudny
fantastic fantastyczny
funny śmieszny
great wspaniały
horrible okropny
their ich
band zespół
pop music muzyka rozrywkowa
pop star gwiazda muzyki rozrywkowej
record płyta
her ja (jej, nią, niej)
him go (jego, jemu, nim)

them ich (im, nimi, nich)
like lubić
think myśleć

LEKCJA 18
gold złoty
or albo, lub
Great! Wspaniale! (wspaniały, wspaniała, wspaniali, wspaniali)
Let's see it. Zobaczmy to
bike rower
camera aparat fotograficzny
football piłka nożna
radio radio
sleeping bag śpiwór
snake wąż
stamp album album ze znaczkami
tennis racket rakieta tenisowa
tent namiot
watch zegarek
wheel koło
over there tam (tam dalej)
one (może oznaczać to samo, co rzeczownik, który zastępuje)
have got mam (masz, mamy, macie, mają)

LEKCJA 19
any jakieś (jakikolwiek, jakikolwiek, jakiś, jakaś, choć trochę, trochę)
foreign zagraniczny
model model
badge naszywka, odznaka, plakietka
coin moneta
collection kolekcja, zbiór
cousin kuzyn, kuzynka
postcard kartka pocztowa
poster plakat
sticker nalepka
train pociąg
How many? Ile?

LEKCJA 20
quiet spokojny, cichy
shy nieśmiały
album album
member członek
sequin cekin
sheep owca
dance tańczę
swap wymieniam
family members członkowie rodziny
aunt ciocia
uncle wujek

LEKCJA 21
altogether razem
Guess what. Wiesz co?
people ludzie
thousand tysiąc
over powyżej (ponad)
under poniżej (pod)
with z

a lot bardzo dużo

LEKCJA 22
best najlepszy
small mały
opposite naprzeciwko
theirs ich
house dom
attic poddasze
bathroom łazienka
bedroom sypialnia
dining room jadalnia
downstairs na dole
floor piętro (podłoga)
ground floor parter
kitchen kuchnia
play room pokój dziecinny (do zabaw)
roof dach
sitting room salonik
toilet toaleta
upstairs na górze

LEKCJA 23
I'm afraid of boję się
alone sam (sama, samo, sami)
dark ciemny
enormous ogromny
full of pełen
private prywatny
spooky niesamowity
because bo, ponieważ
bird's nest gniazdo ptasie
box pudło, pudełko
dolls lalki
flag flaga
game gra
ghost duch
lock zamek
notice wywieszka
photo fotografia
spider pająk
team drużyna
thing rzecz
toy zabawka
typewriter maszyna do pisania
next to obok (tuż obok)
on na
house dom
bed łóżko
box pudło, pudełko
carpet dywan, wykładzina
chimney komin
corner róg
cupboard szafa
curtains firanki
door drzwi
wall ściana
window okno

LEKCJA 24
busy ruchliwy (zajęty)
chalk kreda
historical historyczny
important ważny
interesting ciekawy
large duży
boats statki (łódki)
car ferries promy samochodowe
castle zamek
centre centrum
cliffs urwiska

coast wybrzeże
flower kwiat
garden ogród
hovercraft poduszkowiec
letter list
lighthouse latarnia morska
penfriend kolega, którego zna sie z listów i z którym się koresponduje
place miejsce
port port
remains pozostałości
town miasto
between między, pomiędzy
for ze (z, dla, przez)
near niedaleko
live mieszkam
compass points kierunki geograficzne
east wschód
north północ
north-east północny wschód
north-west północny zachód
south południe
south-east południowy wschód
south-west południowy zachód

LEKCJA 25
quite całkiem
somewhere gdzieś
flat mieszkanie
stairs schody
waiter kelner
into do (do środka)
on the top of na szczycie
over nad
show pokazywać

LEKCJA 26
anything else coś jeszcze
alphabet alfabet
bicycle lamp lampa rowerowa
brush szczotka
capital stolica
comb grzebień
headmaster wychowawca
headmistress wychowawczyni
pair of scissors nożyczki
penknife scyzoryk
president prezydent
purse portmonetka, kosmetyczka
surname nazwisko
torch latarka
wallet portfel
spell literować
want chcieć

LEKCJA 27
sport sport
terrific wspaniały
fast szybko
very well bardzo dobrze
breath oddech
champion mistrz
competition zawody
guitar gitara
hand ręka (dłoń)
head głowa
horse koń

86

omelette omlet
piano pianino, fortepian
rope lina

water woda
can mogę, umiem, potrafię
climb wspinać się
draw rysować
hold wstrzymywać (trzymać)
knit robić na drutach
make robić
move poruszać (ruszać)
play grać
ride jeździć (na koniu, rowerze)
run biegać
send wysyłać
sing śpiewać
speak mówić
stand stać
swim pływać
use używać
walk chodzić

LEKCJA 28
Be quiet! Cicho bądź!
Mind your own business. Pilnuj swego nosa!

girlfriend dziewczyna
hot chocolate czekolada na gorąco
toffee toffi
TV (television) telewizja
do robić (zajmować się)
listen to słuchać (czegoś)
play with bawić się (czymś)
talk to rozmawiać z (kimś)

LEKCJA 29
first pierwszy
last ostatni
second drugi
third trzeci
unlucky pechowy

I don't understand. Nie rozumiem.

ankle kostka (u nogi)
basketball koszykówka
football piłka nożna
leg noga
metre metr
race wyścig
scarf apaszka
tennis tenis
volleyball siatkówka

round dookoła

sit down usiąść (siadać)
stand up wstań (wstawać)
tie wiązać
wear nosić (na sobie)

LEKCJA 30
diamond diament
giant gigantyczny

Scotland Szkocja
Wales Walia
beach plaża
belt pas
birdwatching obserwowanie ptaków
coast guard straż przybrzeżna
gang gang
gun pistolet
island wyspa
lighthouse latarnia morska

packet paczuszka
police policja
puffin maskonurk (ptak wodny)
signal sygnał
smuggler przemytnik
tortoise żółw
village wieś
wetsuit kombinezon płetwonurka

drop rzucić (upuścić)
fall spadać, upaść
fish łowić ryby
fly latać
help pomóżcie (pomoc)
row wiosłować

LEKCJA 31
just tylko (akurat, właśnie)
either również nie
without bez
weigh ważyć (np. ważyć 5 kg)

food jedzenie
Coca-Cola Coca-Cola
apple pie szarlotka
cheeseburger hamburger z serem
chicken kurczak
chips frytki
coffee kawa
cup filiżanka
fish ryba
hamburger hamburger
ketchup ketchup
menu karta potraw
milk mleko
milkshake cocktail mleczny
mustard musztarda
onions cebula
orange juice sok pomarańczowy
pepper pieprz
Pepsi Cola Pepsi Cola
salt sól
strawberry truskawka
tea herbata
tomato soup zupa pomidorowa

LEKCJA 32
nice ładny (miły)
silver srebrny
these (*adj*) te (ci)
those (*adj*) tamte (tamci)

really naprawdę

sports bag sportowa torba

these (*pron*) te (one)
those (*pron*) tamte (one)
Which? Które? (Który?, Która?, Którzy?)

clothes ubrania
roller skates wrotki
shorts szorty
track suit dresy

LEKCJA 33
every każdy (każda, każde)

afternoon popołudnie
break przerwa
lunch obiad
morning rano
subject przedmiot
timetable plan (rozkład zajęć)

weekend wolna sobota, niedziela
When? Kiedy?

days of the week dnie tygodnia

school subjects przedmioty szkolne
Art wychowanie plastyczne
Biology biologia
Computer Studies zajęcia komputerowe
Current Affairs wiedza o społeczeństwie
Drama zajęcia teatralne
French francuski
Games gry sportowe
Geography geografia
History historia
Home Economics prowadzenie domu
Library zajęcia biblioteczne
Maths matematyka
Music muzyka
PE (physical education) wychowanie fizyczne
RE (religious education) religia
Science nauki ścisłe

LEKCJA 34
perfect idealny
neither też nie

activity czynność, zajęcie
adventure przygoda
badminton badminton
free time wolny czas
gymnastics gimnastyka
hole dziura
museum muzeum
plate talerz

by przy, obok

act grać (rolę w przedstawieniu)
canoe kanoe
join dołącz (dołączyć, połączyć, przyłączyć się)
paint malować
put postaw (stawiać)
sail żeglować
scuba dive nurkować z aparatem
ski jeździć na nartach
water ski jeździć na nartach wodnych
windsurf jeździć na desce windsurfingowej

LEKCJA 35
elder starszy
married żonaty (zamężna)
super wspaniały

airport port lotniczy
ambulance driver kierowca karetki pogotowia ratunkowego
customs officer celnik
flavour smak
group grupa
hamburger bar bar hamburgerowy
hospital szpital
physics fizyka

LEKCJA 36
beautiful piękny
cheap tani
clean czysty
clever mądry
dirty brudny
expensive drogi
fat tłusty (tęgi)
friendly przyjacielski
golden złotego koloru
hard twardy (trudny)
long długi
pretty ładny
short krótki (niski wzrostem)
slow powolny
soft miękki, delikatny
thin cienki, chudy
ugly brzydki
unfriendly nieprzyjazny
young młody

a bit odrobinę
sometimes czasami

fur futro
guard stróż (strażnik)
neck szyja
nose nos
shell skorupa
spots plamki
stripes paski
tail ogon

What sort? Jakiego rodzaju?

animals zwierzęta
anteater mrówkojad
giant crab krab gigant
giraffe żyrafa
kitten kociak
koala bear miś koala
Labrador Labrador (pies myśliwski)
leopard lampart (jaguar)
spider monkey małpka pajęczowa
tortoise żółw
zebra zebra

LEKCJA 37
cold zimny
dangerous niebezpieczny
difficult trudny
easy łatwy
frightened przestraszony
heavy ciężki
high wysoki (wysoko)
hot gorący
light lekki
low niski (nisko)
nasty wstrętny
noisy hałaśliwy
safe bezpieczny
next door z domu (mieszkania) obok
quite całkiem

branch gałąź
ladder drabina
someone ktoś

bring przynieść
chase ścigać
get down zejść na dół
hang on zawieś się (przytrzymaj się)
let go puść się (puścić)
reach dosięgnąć
slip poślizgnąć się

LEKCJA 38

happy szczęśliwy
loud szczęśliwy

at first zpoczątku
at last w końcu
clearly wyraźnie, jasno
loudly głośno
nastily wstrętnie
nicely miło
quickly szybko
quietly spokojnie, cicho
slowly wolno
so więc

Wait a moment. Poczekaj chwilkę.

programme program
seat miejsce siedzące
speech przemówienie (mowa)

get dressed ubierać się
go on dalej (rób to dalej)
hear słyszeć
need potrzebować
shut zamknąć
smile uśmiechać się
turn off wyłączyć
welcome przywitać

LEKCJA 39

at least przynajmniej
deep głęboki
exactly dokładnie
far daleko, daleki
more than więcej niż
shallow płytki
special specjalny
tall wysoki
wide szeroki

Gosh! O rany!

bridge most
building budynek
centimetre centymetr
depth głębokość
distance odległość
earth ziemia
end koniec
fact fakt
finger palec
foot/feet stopa/stopy
half pół (połowa)
height wysokość
inch cal
kilometre kilometr
length długość
mile mila
millimetre milimetr
million milion
moon księżyc
mountain góra
ocean ocean
pyramid piramida
quarter ćwierć
river rzeka
swimming pool basen kąpielowy
tower wieża
width szerokość

How (far) (deep)? jak (daleko) (głęboko/i)

LEKCJA 40

either... or albo... albo
fourth czwarty

old-fashioned staromodny
popular popularny
real life prawdziwe życie
rich bogaty
well known dobrze znany

always zawsze

character charakter
soap opera telewizyjny serial obyczajowy

nothing nic

LEKCJA 41

activity (holiday) obozowe (wakacje)
each każdy (każda, każde)
hungry głodny
thirsty spragniony
already już

It's time to go. Czas iść.
Hurry up! Pospiesz się!

holiday wakacje (ferie, święto)
money pieniądze
pence pens
pound funt
price cena
station stacja
week tydzień

something coś

both obydwaj (obydwie, obydwoje)
how much ile

drink pić
eat jeść

food and drink
jedzenie i picie
apple jabłko
biscuit herbatnik
lemonade lemoniada
nut orzech
orange pomarańcz
peach brzoskwinia

LEKCJA 42

bored znudzony
lucky szczęściarz
tired zmęczony

half past wpół do
quarter past kwadrans po
quarter to za kwadrans
tonight dziś wieczór (dziś w nocy)
usually zwykle

bedtime godzina pójścia spać
journey podróż
o'clock 'godzina' (np. 5 o'clock – godzina piąta)
supper kolacja
What time? O której godzinie?

arrive przyjechać

LEKCJA 43

cloudy pochmurno (pochmurny)
dull ponuro (nieciekawie, nieciekawy)
freezing mroźno (mroźny)
sunny słonecznie (słoneczny)
warm ciepło (ciepły)
wet mokro (mokry)

anyway zresztą
on average przeciętnie
hour godzina
lightning błyskawica
rain deszcz
snow śnieg
weather pogoda
behind za
up there tam, w górę (tam, w górze)

go out wyjść
rain padać (o deszczu)
shine świecić
snow padać (o śniegu)

LEKCJA 44

homesick tęskniący za domem

autograph book album z autografami
disco dyskoteka
mini-motorbike miniaturowy motocykl (skuter)
monitor opiekunka
shower prysznic
sort rodzaj

food *jedzenie*
bacon bekon
cereal płatki śniadaniowe
egg jajko
marmalade marmolada
porridge owsianka
sausage kiełbasa
toast grzanka

LEKCJA 45

fine ładny, dobry (w porządku)

cricket krykiet
crop zbiory
farm farma (gospodarstwo rolne)
meal posiłek
season pora roku
spring wiosna
summer lato

die umierać

LEKCJA 46

sad smutny

across w poprzek

aeroplane samolot
cinema kino
lollipop lizak
restaurant restauracja
theatre teatr

lick lizać
mean znaczyć
pronounce wymawiać
sell sprzedawać
sound brzmieć

LEKCJA 47

bossy władczy

autumn jesień
birthday urodziny
calendar kalendarz
card karta
date data
present prezent
winter zima

others inni
collect zbierać
get dostać

months of the year
miesiące roku
ordinal numbers
1st–31st liczebniki porządkowe (pierwszy –trzydziesty pierwszy)

LEKCJA 48

angry zły
crazy zwariowany
lazy leniwy
true prawdziwy
(*It's not true* To nie prawda)

a little trochę

always zawsze
ever kiedykolwiek
never nigdy
often często
sometimes czasami

magazine czasopismo
make-up kosmetyki do makijażu
pocket money kieszonkowe
rubbish śmiecie
truth prawda

believe wierzyć
do the washing up zmywać naczynia
save oszczędzić
spend wydawać (pieniądze)
tidy sprzątać

LEKCJA 49

extra dodatkowy

ballet balet
classical music muzyka poważna
crocodile krokodyl
dictionary słownik
envelope koperta
house plant kwiat doniczkowy
jigsaw układanka
mug kubek
opera opera
rat szczur
scarf szalik
soap mydło
tights rajstopy
writing paper papier listowy (papeteria)

LEKCJA 50

rude grubiański
strange dziwny
technical techniczny
unemployed bez pracy

I don't mind Mnie to nie przeszkadza

course kurs
engineer inżynier (technik)
helmet hełm
night club klub nocny
overall kombinezon roboczy
trainee kursant

laugh at śmiać się z (kogoś)
take for a walk zabrać na spacer

Common irregular verbs

These verbs are in their infinitive/past tense/past participle forms.

VERBS WITH NO CHANGE

cost	cost	cost
cut	cut	cut
hit	hit	hit
let	let	let
put	put	put
shut	shut	shut

VERBS WITH ONE CHANGE

bring	brought	brought
build	built	built
buy	bought	bought
catch	caught	caught
feel	felt	felt
find	found	found
get	got	got
hang	hung	hung
have	had	had
hear	heard	heard
hold	held	held
keep	kept	kept
learn	learnt	learnt
leave	left	left
lend	lent	lent
lose	lost	lost
make	made	made
mean	meant	meant
meet	met	met
pay	paid	paid
read	read	read
say	said	said
sell	sold	sold
send	sent	sent
shine	shone	shone
sit	sat	sat
sleep	slept	slept
spell	spelled/spelt	spelled/spelt
spend	spent	spent
stand	stood	stood
tell	told	told
think	thought	thought
understand	understood	understood
win	won	won

VERBS WITH TWO CHANGES

be	was	been
begin	began	begun
break	broke	broken
choose	chose	chosen
come	came	come
do	did	done
draw	drew	drawn
drink	drank	drunk
drive	drove	driven
eat	ate	eaten
fall	fell	fallen
fly	flew	flown
forget	forgot	forgotten
give	gave	given
go	went	gone
grow	grew	grown
know	knew	known
lie	lay	lain
ride	rode	ridden
ring	rang	rung
run	ran	run
see	saw	seen
show	showed	shown
sing	sang	sung
speak	spoke	spoken
steal	stole	stolen
swim	swam	swum
take	took	taken
wear	wore	worn
write	wrote	written

Songs

LESSON 5 **Come along now**

Come along now
And meet your partners.
Move your desk and chairs.
Come along now
And greet your partners.
Move your desk and chairs.

Take a seat
And face your partners.
It's fun to work in pairs.
Ask for names
And ask for numbers.
It's fun to work in pairs.
It's fun to work in pairs.

Come along now
And meet your partners.
Move your desk and chairs.
Come along now
And greet your partners.
Move your desk and chairs.

Take a seat
And face your partners.
It's fun to work in pairs.
Ask more questions
Get more answers.
It's fun to work in pairs
It's fun to work in pairs.

Come along now
And meet your partners.
Move your desk and chairs.
Come along now
And greet your partners.
Move your desk and chairs.

LESSON 9 **Save the tiger**

Save the tiger.
Save the whale and the panda.
Save the tiger.
Save the whale and the gorilla.
Save the elephant in Africa
The eagle in America.
Save the wildlife of the world.
Save the tiger!

LESSON 14 **People of today**

She's a woman of today
On the TV screen,
Selling frozen food
Or French icecream.
With her grey-green eyes
And shining hair
Her perfect teeth
And skin so fair
She's a perfect woman of today.
She's a perfect woman of today.

He's a man of today
In a magazine,
Selling aftershave
Or margarine.
He's got dark brown eyes
And a lovely tan
And the sort of looks
That make a man
Look handsome in a very modern way,
Look handsome in a very modern way.

She's a woman of today
On the TV screen,
Selling frozen food
Or French icecream.
He's a man of today
In a magazine
Selling aftershave
Or margarine.
They're perfect people of today.
They're perfect people of today.

LESSON 30 **Funny family**

Oh, what a family.
What a funny family.
Oh, what a funny family!
We haven't any money
But we're really very funny.
And we're happy, just as happy as can be.
Happy, just as happy as can be.

My mother
Is a kung fu teacher.
They call her China tea.
My dad
Is a lighthouse keeper,
Out in the middle of the sea.
My granny's
In a cupboard in the garden.
Sister Susie
Wears a cabbage on her head.
Brother Charlie
Keeps his money in a bucket.
Uncle Harry
Keeps a python in his bed.

Oh, what a family.
What a funny family.
Oh, what a funny family!
We haven't any money
But we're really very funny.
And we're happy, just as happy as can be.
Happy, just as happy as can be.

Longman Group UK Limited
Longman House, Burnt Mill, Harlow,
Essex CM20 2JE, England
and Associated Companies throughout the world.

© Brian Abbs and Ingrid Freebairn 1986

All rights reserved. No part of this publication may be reproduced, stored in a retrieval system, or transmitted in any form or by any means, electronic, mechanical, photocopying, recording, or otherwise, without the prior written permission of the Copyright owner.

First published 1986
This edition first published 1992
Second impression 1992

ISBN 0 582 10252 9

Designed by Nucleus design Associates
Illustrated by Chris Ryley,
with Michael Stafford, Julie Tennent, Andrew Aloof, Tony Ross, Peter Dennis, Tony Kenyon

Set in Scantext Palatino
Printed in Hong Kong
GC/02

The publishers would like to point out that all characters in the book are completely fictitious.

Acknowledgements

The authors and publishers would like to thank the following for their invaluable comments on the manuscript: Luciano Mariani, Serena Pasinetti, Eddie Edmundson, Regina Guimaráes, Janet Dangar, Marisol Valcarcel, Mercedes Verdú, Mercedes López de Blas, Ana Okamika, Ana Fernandez, Antony Loproto.

We are grateful to D C Thomson & Co Ltd for permission to reproduce an adapted version of the article '24 hours with Anne McCrodden' from *Jackie* magazine no 1074 (4/8/84).

We are grateful to the following for permission to reproduce copyright photographs:

Ace Photo Agency/Paul Craven for page 20 (bottom left inset); All-Sport Photographic Ltd for page 46 (top left) & 46 (bottom left); Art Directors Photo Library for pages 13 (top middle) & 18 (right); Associated Sports Photography for page 46 (top right); Bob Thomas Sports Photography for page 46 (bottom right); British Tourist Authority for pages 53 (top left) & 71 (left); Bruce Coleman Ltd for page 58 (middle right); Camera Press Ltd for pages 6 (top middle) 13 (top right), 19 (bottom), 58 (top middle), 58 (middle left), 58 (bottom left) & 58 (bottom right); The J. Allan Cash Photo Library for pages 19 (bottom inset), 20 (top right inset) & 68 (top left); Colorific!/Mary Ellen Mark/Visages for page 17 (right); Colorific!/B. Bartholomew for page 31; Daily Telegraph Colour Library for page 10 (middle); David Redfern Photography for page 6 (bottom right); European Design Partnership for page 57 (top); Geoff Morgan Photography for page 68 (top right); Image Bank/Gerald Brimacombe for page 20 (bottom right inset); The John Hillelson Agency Ltd/SYGMA for page 63 (top); Leo Mason Photo Library for pages 17 (middle) & 46 (top middle); Licensiado Jose Agasto for page 23; Longman Photographic Unit for pages 10 (bottom), 25-26, 65 & 67; Marion & Tony Morrison South American Pictures for page 19 (top inset); Anders Mathlein for page 55; Reproduced by permission of the National Postal Museum for page 16 (top right); Photo Library International-Leeds for page 68 (bottom left); Pictor International-London for pages 13 (bottom middle) & 58 (top right); Pictorial Press Ltd for page 27 (middle right), 27 (bottom left) & 27 (bottom right); Picturepoint-London for pages 10 (top), 19 (top), 20 (top left inset), 20 (top left), 20 (top right), 20 (bottom left), 20 (bottom right), 37, 53 (top middle), 53 (top right), 53 (bottom left), 57 (bottom) & 71 (right); Graham Portlock for pages 65/66 (bottom); RETNA Pictures Ltd for page 27 (top left); Rex Features Ltd for pages 6 (bottom middle), 17 (left), 18 (upper middle) & 18 (middle); Rogers & Cowan, Inc. for page 27 (top right); Chris Ryley for page 57 (middle); Syndication International Library for page 18 (top) & 18 (left); By arrangement with D.C. Thomson & Co. Ltd. © D.C. Thomson & Co. Ltd 1984 for page 79; Tim Graham Picture Library for page 6 (top left), 6 (top right) & 6 (bottom left); Tony Stone Photo Library-London for page 13 (top left), 13 (bottom left), 13 (bottom right), 24, 53 (bottom right) & 58 (top left); Topham Picture Library for pages 63 (bottom) & 68 (bottom right); © 1984 Tritec Music Ltd. under licence to EMI Records/Francesco Scavulla for page 27 (middle); Reprinted with the permission of Wimpy International Limited for page 49 (right).